🦅 *Seasons Without Shade*

![Photo](tornado cleanup)

Photo courtesy of Star Tribune.

Seasons

WITHOUT

Shade

Edited by Chad Thomas

Photo courtesy of St. Paul Pioneer Press.

✒ Contents

Dedicated to the people of the Siren area,
who've shown they're not just victims, but also survivors.

And in loving memory of the three people killed by the tornado:
Tom Haseltine, Ruth Schultz and Sylvan Stellrecht.

About This Book

There's a certain amount of therapy that comes in sharing life's tragic moments with others. A sense that everyone is in this together. Never was that more true than in the tiny northwestern Wisconsin community of Siren, where a fierce twister bore down on June 18, 2001. Three people were killed, and many others injured. The tornado also leveled homes and businesses, tearing people's lives apart in the process.

But truly the most remarkable part of the story is what came out of the rubble. Thanks to an unbelievable outpouring of community support, the town quickly began picking up the pieces—putting the scattered puzzle back together again.

This book is, first, an account from community members of the night when strong winds changed life in Siren forever. Beyond that, and perhaps more importantly, an attempt to convey the community spirit that grew and blossomed in the days and weeks after the tornado.

This book is a collaboration in the truest sense of the word. To start with, the idea for it was not mine, but Siren resident Luanne Swanson's. It was Luanne who marshaled the troops, recruiting people to go out and interview community members about their experiences. This book would not have been possible without Luanne's dedication, and that of the other volunteers who gave their time to collect the stories: Barb Lyga, Nancy Daniels, Nancy Jappe, and Jill Gloodt. I am so proud of the work these women did. They put in long hours to collect and write the stories in this book. Ladies, we made it!

Throughout all of our discussions, Dave Tripp was also there, both offering advice and assuring everyone that this was, in fact, a great idea. And after we compiled the book, it was Dave who made sure it actually made it to the printing press. Without him, this dream would surely have never become a reality.

Many thanks also to the people at the Inter-County Leader, who opened their news and photo archives for this project. The Star Tribune and Saint Paul Pioneer Press in the Twin Cities also graciously provided photos that appear on these pages. And when Lakeland Press in Siren learned we were writing this book, the owner agreed to reprint photos for us for free. Clare Erickson with the New Richmond Historical Society loaned us her copy of *The New Richmond Cyclone* published in

1899 that we excerpted in this book. The Burnett County Historical Society also provided us with information to put this story into historical context.

Thanks to Janet Thomas for typing many of the stories, as well as Amy Swanson, who did some writing and typing for us.

Many thanks fo Bernice Abrahamzon for proofreading this book, adding her set of experienced eyes to its pages. The biggest thanks goes to the people of the Siren area, who, after already enduring so much media attention, agreed to talk once again for this project.

Everyone involved with this book donated his or her time, so that any profit from it could go back to the Siren community. At our many meetings, we discussed at length what to do with the proceeds. And after realizing one of the things many of us most missed were Siren's large, mature trees, we decided the money would go toward restoring the town's woodsy feel by purchasing trees and paying for other beautification projects.

Thanks to the hard work and perseverance of all Siren residents, we WILL be back, better than ever

—*Chad Thomas, Book Editor*

Seasons Without Shade

SIREN

SIREN –1916– Viewed from atop Soo Line windmill. L. to R. Tjader's (J.-B. Hanson's later), Nelson's, Hotel Complex, Shorrocks' Store (Blom's after fire), First Post Office Building (John E. Maloney, Postmaster), Bengt Olson's and upper left is the top of Blom's Store & "The Opera House" Hall topside.

Courtesy of Burnett County Historical Society.

Before the Tornado

"They liked New Richmond for the beauty of its location; the magnificent trees; the calm serenity by which they were surrounded . . ."

— Mary Adeline Boehm, June 12, 1899
The New Richmond Cyclone

About 80 miles from Minneapolis and Saint Paul, the Siren area is surrounded by some of northwestern Wisconsin's best lakes and woodland. The area's dense forests and abundant wildlife first drew immigrants to the area from Sweden in the 1880s.

The town's first post office dates back to 1890, built about one mile north of the present village. It's thanks to the abundant lilacs that bloomed around that first location that Siren got its name. C.O. Segerstrom, the first postmaster, liked the lilacs so much, he chose the Swedish word for lilac, Syren, for the new community's name. The name was eventually Americanized, switched to the present day Siren.

In 1903, early settlers moved the town to the shores of Little Doctor's Lake, about a mile west of the present location. By this time, Siren had grown to include businesses such as a creamery, blacksmith shop and dance hall. And pioneering merchant Edwin Nelson built his first mercantile at this site as well.

In 1912, the Soo Line Railroad was extended from Frederic (10 miles south of Siren) up to Duluth, connecting the entire area to the Twin Cities. This was the reason the village moved to its present-day site. The town's merchants wanted to be close to the railway line and the commerce it brought with it. Edwin Nelson was the first to build on Siren's Main Street, which was then just a block long. Nelson's Store quickly became a mainstay of the community, as it would remain for decades. Even in the late 1970s, Nelson's Store was still a general store, providing clothing, shoes, material and a host of household goods. Today, the building houses a gift shop and clothing store.

In those pioneering days, families planted themselves in Siren and put down roots that took hold. Very early on, many familiar names to Siren had already arrived in the community. Along with the Nelsons, there were the Tjaders, Swensons, Nybergs, Dahlbergs, Olsons, Engstroms and Daniels. (Descendents of those families, and of many other early pioneers, still live in the Siren area today—creating a tight-knit community.)

In 1932, the village of Siren had its first brush with disaster. A fire in February of that year swept through much of the downtown, destroying a hardware store, bakery, pool hall, garage and grocery store. All the buildings but two were completely destroyed on that side of

Main Street. But no lives were lost, and Siren residents quickly set to the task of rebuilding their burnt up little community. By 1937, five years after the fire and 25 years after the village moved to its present location, community members held a huge, three-day Silver Jubilee celebration to mark the progress the community had made. At this time, the village's population had soared to 300.

Decades later, on June 18, 2001, Siren residents were again put to the test. More than 100 years after those first settlers put Siren on the map, a deadly twister, the kind rarely seen in the Midwest, nearly took it off.

The National Weather Service first spotted touchdown of the tornado at 8:06 P.M. about 13 miles west/northwest of Siren. As it traveled toward the town, it passed through the unincorporated communities of Alpha and Falun. By 8:20 P.M., the F3 twister, with wind speeds gusting over 200 miles an hour, hit Siren. The tornado continued on a route to the east for many more miles, finally lifting back up off the ground and into the clouds three miles west of Spooner, Wisconsin, around 9 P.M.

In all, the tornado spent 54 minutes on the ground, leaving behind a 34-mile-long path of destruction. At its widest point, the twister stretched for half a mile. More than 51,000 acres of land had at least some damage. The figures for other destruction were just as staggering: 175 buildings destroyed, 177 more with major damage and 198 with minor damage. But without doubt, the greatest tragedy was the human toll the tornado took. Three people died as a result of the twister, another 16 were injured.

Just as they had after the 1932 fire, in the hours and days after the tornado Siren residents rose to the challenge, reaching out to neighbors and strangers alike. More than 15,000 people came from around the region, and other parts of the country, to help clean up. Many more donated hundreds of thousands of dollars for victims. In the end, people learned valuable lessons about themselves, and discovered an even greater appreciation for their small town than they had already known.

—*Chad Thomas, Book Editor*

The Tornado Strikes

"Instead of home, comforts, luxuries and happiness, chaos reigned supreme on this unfortunate spot of Mother Earth."

—Mary Adeline Boehm, June 12, 1899
The New Richmond Cyclone

Photo courtesy of Star Tribune.

A Reporter's Notebook

"As a reporter, you become conditioned to seeing destruction. You try to divorce your own thoughts about what you're seeing, from the job you have to do. But as I wandered around Siren that night, it was impossible for me to concentrate."

—*Chad Thomas, Reporter and Former Siren Resident*

By Chad Thomas

It was a sunny and warm Monday morning. Perfect weather for a jog. I had gotten up a little bit late, but on such a nice day I was determined to get in a run on the quiet back roads around my parents' home before heading to work for the afternoon shift. So I quickly laced up my running shoes and headed out the door.

Running has always been a physical and mental release for me. A time to reflect on the past, and ponder the future. On this particular outing I was thinking about the past year and half living in Duluth, Minnesota. I had moved there in October 1999 to work as a television news reporter, fulfilling a dream of mine since eighth grade.

Just prior to my time in Duluth, I had spent two years overseas. As much as living in other countries had intrigued me, I had come home because I was tired of that exotic life and wanted to be closer to my family and old friends. My time in Duluth had accomplished just that. In fact, I was in my hometown of Siren, Wisconsin, Monday morning because I had come down from Duluth the previous day for a Father's Day BBQ at my parents' house.

After my jog I quickly showered, dressed and jumped in the car to get to work on time. As I headed for Duluth, I had to drive through Siren. Looking around I realized that the town I grew up in had changed a lot while I had been away.

Over the past few years the community of 900 had seen something of a building boom: two new hotels, a movie theatre, a specialty coffee shop, gift stores, a new restaurant and indoor ice rink. Owners of many of the older, established businesses had also remodeled, or torn down their buildings and started over from scratch. Even Siren's K-12 school had gotten a facelift, with major renovations and additions to handle the growing student population. In short, Siren was in the midst of a renaissance, and as I drove out of town I thought for a minute about how proud I was of the community's growth.

I often spent weekends frequenting many of the new businesses that had sprouted up here, and stopping in at the old establishments I had been visiting since I was a kid. These were familiar surroundings—surroundings that in only a matter of hours would be dramatically altered.

That afternoon I was putting together a story on the last minute discussions of the Duluth School District's budget. The district was in the midst of a financial crisis, trying to cope with a several-million-dollar shortfall. After months of debate, the vote on the coming year's budget was set for Tuesday. I had covered the story all year, and quite frankly was more than ready for the final decision.

I had just finished writing my piece for the 10 P.M. news, when the weather alerts began coming into the newsroom—prompting my station's chief meteorologist, Phil Johnson, to break into programming with bulletins on the worsening weather conditions. Around 7:45 P.M., Phil came over to my desk and urged me to call my parents, telling me it appeared a tornado was headed right for my hometown. I tried, but couldn't reach them.

By 8 P.M., the warnings were getting continually more ominous. Finally, an alert came across the weather wire telling people to take cover immediately from the powerful tornado. The wording removed any doubt from Phil's mind about the magnitude of the storm.

"The language was at a level that I rarely have seen," Phil would later tell me, "so that immediately indicated to me that this was a very dangerous situation." Throughout the evening, Phil would continue cutting into regular programming with updated information on the powerful storm, knowing people's lives might be at stake.

I left a couple of minutes after that first critical bulletin with photojournalist Aaron Goodyear, racing right toward Siren, the heart of the storm. As we made our way south out of

Superior, Wisconsin, toward Siren, we encountered some heavy rain and a little wind, but nothing too serious. In fact, when we got to the halfway point between Superior and Siren, an unincorporated area known as Moose Junction, it appeared that maybe the storm hadn't been as bad as we had first thought. It was completely calm. The skies were light. The sun was even peeking out.

But between live cut-ins on the air, Phil was updating us on our cell phone, letting us know that there were confirmed reports of a tornado in the Siren area, and that weather conditions were ripe for more tornadoes. At one point, one of our sportscasters, Chris Long, got on the phone, grimly reminding us no news story was worth our lives.

By 9:45 P.M. we had reached the Burnett County Government Center, located 2 miles north of Siren. Our cell phone was no longer working. With only 15 minutes until the 10 P.M. news, we decided to stop there to get whatever information we could about the tornado, and hopefully find a phone to use.

We managed to locate Burnett County Sheriff Tim Curtin, who filled us in on what he knew at that point. He also let us use a phone to broadcast this report for the 10 P.M. news:

> *"Well Pat, that's right. I am about two miles north of Siren at the Burnett County Sheriff's office. We have actually not been able to go into Siren yet at this point because currently the sheriff's department has the area cordoned off.*
>
> *Sheriff—Burnett County Sheriff Tim Curtin tells us that there is extensive damage to the village of Siren. There are a number of buildings that have been damaged. Trees are*

down. *They are getting reports of gas leaks in the area, as well as a number of power lines being down. Phone service and power is out throughout the region. At this point, they're saying that they're getting reports of minor injuries. Nothing too extensive to report, thankfully, in that area.*

There's also reports of a lot of damage in this area in the rural parts of the county. There are barns that have been blown down. And farmers have said that they have had to put down some of their livestock that has been damaged from the storm.

The sheriff's department currently has six or seven ambulances out. They also have called in all their off-duty officers and have crews scattered throughout the region. They're asking people to stay away from the village of Siren at this hour so that crews can get in there and assess the damage to the village.

That's the very latest from here, we'll toss it back to you in the studio."

I had still not been into Siren, and after filing my 10 P.M. story was anxious to see the town myself. But the sheriff's department had blocked all traffic from entering on the highway north of town. Determined to get in, we started down some of the back roads that led into Siren. This is where we got our first look at the devastation left in the twister's path.

It was a chaotic scene.

The roads were impassible, covered by trees and power lines. Homes were blown apart. The entire area, without electricity, was pitch black. Stunned residents were wandering up and down the road wondering who was alive, and who was dead. As would be the case over the coming days, I kept running into people I knew. And all of them were saying the same thing: Siren was gone.

As more and more people told me about the utter devastation, I was getting more and more worried about my own family. With the phone lines knocked out, I still hadn't been able to reach my parents. I hadn't heard anything from my sister and her husband, Bob and Heather O'Brien, either. And unlike my parents, who lived five miles east of Siren, Bob and Heather lived right in town.

There was no way I was going to leave without reaching my family and seeing the destruction in town for myself. But getting into Siren from the back roads we were on proved impossible. And after coming within inches of driving right into a downed power line, Aaron and I decided to turn around and head back toward the highway. When we got there, sheriff's deputies still had the road closed.

I was getting frantic at this point and decided to try another way into Siren, telling Aaron to drive down this old railroad bed that ran right into town. It had been converted into a hiking trail, and the tracks had long since been torn out.

As we got closer to town, we parked the truck and began walking. Once we reached the north side of Siren, we carefully crossed a ditch filled with water. As I looked around at this part of town, which I had driven past just twelve hours earlier, I was completely lost. The devastation was so bad, I honestly wasn't exactly sure of my location at first.

Finally I was able to get my bearings when Aaron found a trophy case. We were right where the new hockey rink had once stood. It was inconceivable to me that this massive structure was gone—completely. The only thing there now, a few twisted heaps of metal. It was now about 11:30 P.M.

During the 10 P.M. news earlier that night, I had done my report without actually seeing Siren with my own eyes, relying instead on information from the Burnett County Sheriff's Department. At that time, I had worried about making the situation seem worse than it was. Now as I surveyed the scene for myself, I kept thinking the devastation was more severe than I ever could have imagined.

As a reporter, you become conditioned to seeing destruction. You try to divorce your own thoughts about what you're seeing, from the job you have to do. But as I wandered around Siren that night, it was impossible for me to concentrate. This was my hometown. The people I talked to I had known for years, some my entire life. I could see the office where my mom worked had been torn apart. My concerns became less focused on putting together a story for the news, and more on finding out what had happened to friends and family. By this point, I still hadn't heard anything from my parents, or my sister and her husband.

As Aaron and I walked toward the center of town, the emergency command center stood out in the darkness—like God's beacon calling his scattered flock in from the darkness. Large floodlights bathed the parking lot of Main Street Market. Dozens had gathered there asking what they could do to help. It was organized chaos. Light from the command center glowed in the tops of the few remaining trees. The scene was otherworldly.

By 3 A.M. I was exhausted—both physically and mentally. But there were live reports to prepare for the 6 A.M. news. And so I started writing. Like many others, I was running on pure adrenaline. As I was scribbling away, a photographer from WCCO Television in Minneapolis came up to me, and told me he had run into my father; my dad had told him to let me know everyone in my family was okay. I breathed a sigh of relief and thanked him for the good news. I was anxious to see them.

As the sun came up that next morning, I went on the air to tell the people of the Northland what had happened to my little hometown. Siren residents were wandering around, getting their first chance to begin assessing the true severity of the damage. What we all saw looked like a war zone. All the trees were gone on the north end of town. Buildings were blown apart. Cars littered the streets. Helicopters from the Twin Cities television stations hovered overhead, adding to the warlike feeling.

As I finished up on the air, my mom and sister came walking up. I was so happy to see both of them. I gave them a big hug.

That morning as I walked around, I felt very conflicted. There was no place I would rather have been. In fact, no one could have kept me away from Siren. But I wished I were helping clean up—not asking people for interviews. I wondered, "Is this harder or easier for people to have someone they know asking them questions about the tornado?" I tried to convince myself it was easier.

That day many of my Channel 3 colleagues came to Siren to help with our coverage—our newscasts were filled with reports from Siren. I felt fortunate to be working with true professionals, all of whom gave 110 percent to get the word out that Siren had been hit, and that the town needed help cleaning up.

That evening I stayed at my parents' house.

Except for a one-hour nap, I had not slept for 36 hours. I fell into bed exhausted.

Over the next two days, I stayed in Siren, filing reports for Channel 3. Thursday we did another live broadcast from town, this one focused on building hope. I did a story that day with Siren Pastor Diane Blahauvietz. When I got off the air that night, I looked around town at all the devastation. As I sat there talking to my sister, Heather, tears rolled down my face. "Our little town will never be the same," I told her.

Later, I was talking to one of our news anchors, and a respected colleague of mine, Amy Rutledge, about how upset and worried I was. She looked at me, and in her stern, but caring way, told me I had to believe the stories I was writing about hope and rebirth.

She was right. As I sit here tonight, nearly four months after the tornado, finishing this book, I can see the town is bouncing back. And I have no doubt, after reading all the stories from the people of Siren, that I grew up in a special place. Once you've read them, I'm sure you'll feel the same.

Holding on for Dear Life

> "The winds were so strong, that they pulled him straight out from the pole. He hung there and watched as the barn blew up."
>
> —*Virginia Hennessey, talking about what happened to her husband*

By Virginia Hennessey

My husband, Joe Hennessey, and I purchased our farm in Alpha on Highway 70 across from the Burnett Dairy Co-op 13 years ago. We moved to the farm because we wanted our sons, Shane and John, to have the opportunity to grow up on a farm and learn good work ethics. (Alpha is about 9 miles west of Siren.)

After years of work, by June of 2001 we had finally gotten the farm to the point where all we had to do was maintain it. We had remodeled a 19th century hand-hewn log home that was on the farm but was previously uninhabitable. This took us three years to renovate. We made it into a bed and breakfast, and named it Smoland Prairie Homestead Inn. We wanted people to come and stay on our small farm, and learn about a life that comes from the soil. We sold antiques and other things in the Granary, Garden Shop, Horse Barn and Santa Shop. The Horse Barn and Santa Shop were completed June 1, 2001.

Then June 18 came, and our lives and business changed forever. I work in the Twin Cities, staying there four nights during the week. I had just arrived at my brother's house after work, and heard there were tornado warnings for the Grantsburg area (Grantsburg is 15 miles west of Siren). I tried to call home many times but was unable to get through. I told my brother I was going to drive home. (He told me not to, but I had to get home.) As I was driving on Interstate 35 approaching the Grantsburg/Highway 70 exit, I was listening to WCCO Radio in the Twin Cities. People tracking the storm were calling in to report what was going on in different places.

One guy got on the radio and said he had just gone through Grantsburg and didn't see any damage there. But he was now in Alpha, and said the co-op was hit hard. Bins and trucks were turned over. The farm across the highway from the co-op had all the trees blown down. He said he could hear them shooting animals. My heart went to my feet. I knew that was our farm. I drove 90 miles an hour the rest of the way.

When I got to Alpha, I had been going so fast that I even drove past our driveway and had to turn around at the dairy. I drove up the driveway; all the trees were down but I could still get up to the house. There were already many people there. Two cows were dead in the driveway. I couldn't see anything so I just yelled, "Where is everyone?" I started to walk around the trees to get to the house.

My son, Shane, yelled back, "Stay where you are. I will come and get you." Then I fell in a hole where a tree had been uprooted.

When Shane came to me, I started to cry and said, "Is everyone ok?"

He replied, "We are fine; some of the horses and cows are hurt."

We were all standing there, looking around at everything that had happened. It was unbelievable that all this could happen in just seconds. All 20 trees around the house, the hay barn and horse barn were damaged. The roof was torn off the Bed and Breakfast. The porch on our house was pushed off its foundation. Many other things were just gone.

But we were still blessed. Everyone was alive. My husband, Joe, sons, Shane and John, and John's girlfriend, Kelly Sandstrom, had just put the horses in the barn before the storm hit. John and Kelly were in their car on their way down the driveway, when they saw the tornado coming. John stepped on the gas to get out onto the highway. The wind was so strong, it pushed their car across the highway and into the ditch. Joe wasn't able to make it into the house, so he grabbed onto a pole in our yard. The winds were so strong, that they pulled him straight out from the pole. He hung there and watched as the barn blew up. The cows were on the east side of the barn, and Joe saw one of the cows fly right over the silo. All within a matter of seconds!

Joe thought John and Kelly might not have made it. He could hear the animals crying. He ran to find John and Kelly and check on the animals. John and Kelly meantime were able to get out of the ditch, and the first thing John said to Kelly was," I hope it missed the farm." But as they drove up the driveway, they knew the farm had been hit badly. John yelled for his dad, but there was no answer. They ran up to what was left of the horse barn. When John finally found Joe, he ran and put his hands on his dad and said, "You're alive." Joe turned around and replied, "Oh, you both are alive." They all hugged.

Then Joe told our son to get a gun and shoot any animals that were hurt beyond help. There wasn't enough time to wait for a veterinarian. In no time, people were showing up from all over to help. Neighbors, Kenny and Dawn Luke, came and took the three horses hurt the worst to their place, so the vet would be able to come and look at them. We later found out that our Arabian stud colt had to be put down. He would never have been able to walk again.

After everyone had left around 2:00 A.M., Joe and I walked around the farm. We could not believe what we saw. Devastation and death were all around us. Our beloved horses and cows were entangled in fences, severely wounded and dying. Trees were uprooted, an antique cutter sleigh demolished, the roof on most of the outbuildings gone, the walls and windows smashed. We went back to the house and tried to get some rest, but were unable to sleep. At 4:30 A.M. I got up to make coffee. Then Joe got up and started to take pictures. We were not sure when the insurance company would be able to make it to our house.

By 5:30, there were already at least 20 men and women (who had taken off from their jobs) at our farm to help. They had chain saws, bobcats, and equipment to help cut up all the trees. By 3:00 that afternoon, all the trees and branches were already in a huge pile on the side of the farm. Others came after they finished at their jobs to help put tarps on the log house, which had lost its roof. We don't know what we would have done without all the help. It also gave us the strength to continue on each day and begin rebuilding.

People brought over everything imaginable—food, bottled water, tools, wheelbarrows, gloves, boxes. We just couldn't believe how people came to our aid after the tornado. People would tell us how sorry they were, and then give us a hug and start to cry. I would have to tell them, "Please don't cry because if I start to cry, I may never stop." We just didn't have time to feel sorry for ourselves. There was just too much to do. (And I suppose I hid a lot of feelings by keeping busy.)

For days after the tornado, we would get up at dawn and work until dark. We learned there were people from all over coming up to Siren to help, and some of them were getting turned away from the town, ending up at our place. We took all the help we could get. Joe and I would often wonder each day, "Where do we start?" So each morning over coffee, we made a list of the things we wanted, and needed, to get done that day. Believe it or not, by dark the list was complete. We had to box up everything in the bed and breakfast so that Larry Merriefield, our carpenter, could start repairing it. We rented a tractor-trailer, which was set up right in the front yard for 3 months until the log home was fixed.

By Sunday, June 24th, we had most of the clean up done. Monday, June 25th, Wayne Lake and his crew were there to clean up the rest of the mess. The people from General Mills, where I work in the Twin Cities, were there to assist in any way they could. They also put together a storm fund for us. We were able to buy 15 big trees and plant them June 24th. By Monday morning, the birds were coming back to our yard and sitting on the small branches.

It was a wonderful sight to see from our badly damaged porch, which the tornado had knocked off its foundation. All the screens were also out, and the things on the porch, either broken or tossed around inside. The porch was the first thing we had to repair. Darcy Stark was able to start work on it Monday, June 25th. This was the place where we were able to feed everyone working at our farm. Even without the screens, people could still come here to take a break and get out of the hot sun.

Burnett Dairy, where Joe works, gave us bottled water, along with cheese and meat trays, for the workers. The Country Cafe in Grantsburg fixed lunch and dinner for us several days during the week.

As the weeks go by, we continue to pick up. The bed and breakfast will be open again October 1st. We have a shed built for our cows. We are building a big pole barn for all the horses, hay, feed and tractors. We know in our heart that God does things for a reason. We are still not sure why this happened, but we will be able to see it is some day.

We moved to the farm to give our boys the opportunity to grow and learn. We know it was a lot of work for them. Joe and I came from a non-farming background, and tried to start a dairy farm. We did a lot of things right, and many wrong. We sure learned a lot. We no longer have dairy cows, only beef now. One thing I do know for sure as we try to start over, our boys have grown into really nice men. They have been there to help us pick up the pieces and rebuild. It will be a sad thing if more small family farms are not around anymore.

We also wanted to rebuild so our grandchildren would be able to come to the farm. Even our one granddaughter now has learned to work right alongside me. Her name is Harlei Hennessey, and she loves to bake with me in the kitchen, too. Harlei has also watched people come and go through the log home. She was there while we were fixing it up, having tea parties with her dolls and bears.

Unimaginable Devastation

"How are we going to save my husband's herd from under the barn rubble?"

—*Lylea Meyer, Farmer*

By Barb Lyga

Lylea Meyer and her husband, John, understand quite well that we all live at mother nature's mercy. For 20 years, they've operated a dairy farm in the Falun area, west of Siren. As farmers, they need to be very in tune with the earth, taking their cue from the weather on when to plant and harvest.

They liked making a living off the land. It was often a gamble, but they got to be the boss. They ran a typical family farm, with a barn, silo, three corncribs and two storage sheds. They grew corn, soybeans and alfalfa on their 350 acres—much of it to feed their 36 milk cows and five heifers. The Meyers had raised three of their four children there. And they now had three grandchildren.

The night of the tornado, they saw a green and black sky in the north. The west was clear. Their neighbor, Al Byers, called to tell them a storm was on the way. John had also heard warnings on the radio. Despite their understanding of nature, they did not sense what was about to come. But when it started getting windy, Lylea headed to the basement. John and their two boys waited to take cover until

they saw big round hay bales lifting off the field. Soon they heard a whoosh noise. It was the windows breaking. It all lasted only two minutes at most.

"What a mess," Lylea thought, after she emerged from the basement. Looking at the extent of the damage, she worried about her 19-year-old daughter Courtney, wondering where she was. Courtney had been at her boyfriend's house in Frederic, south of Siren. Lylea went right out to the truck and used her cell phone to try and reach Courtney at her boyfriend's. To Lylea's relief, Courtney was there. She had tried to come home, but had gone back because of the storm. Soon after that, the phone went dead. At least she knew her daughter was alive and well.

Next Lylea turned her attention toward the cows. The barn was leveled, and most of her herd was trapped there. She wondered: "How are we going to save my husband's herd from under the barn rubble?" The sad answer: Many couldn't. As they dug through the rubble that night, they were simply too badly wounded. It hit Lylea and John hard when they had to put down that first injured cow. It was a scene that would be repeated many times that night, as they worked using flashlights and headlights from the tractors. Only 12 of the 36 cows in the barn survived. Eight had to be put down; 16 were already dead. They never found the five heifers that had been in the pasture. They had blown away in the storm, vanishing forever.

The next day was also very busy. Many people came to help, bringing tractors, bobcats and backhoes. Lots of tears rolled down Lylea's face. She had such mixed emotions. She was devastated by what had happened, and at the same time grateful for all the assistance.

The storm, Lylea says, has brought her family closer together. She also has a greater appreciation for life and other people. She'll never forget all the groups that came from as far away as the Twin Cities to help out. Total strangers brought their trucks, chainsaws, shovels and manpower. "With them we cleaned up," Lylea says. "And there was hope and laughter that day despite the work and heat. People have big hearts, and they really supported each other through all of this."

A Gift From The Tornado

"It could have been worse. I could have been a widow."

—*Janis Wegner, Siren Resident*

By Nancy Jappe

A perfect stranger living more than 80 miles from Siren had a special gift for Dave and Janis Wegner. Gilbert Wald—whose home is north of Cable, Wisconsin—had an 8 x 10 picture of the Wegners' oldest son, Wesley, taken when he was in the sixth grade at Siren Elementary School. What made this unique was that Wald found the picture in his driveway, soon after the June 18 tornado hit and destroyed the Wegners' two-story home and Dave's nearby cabinet shop.

When the Wegners last saw the picture, it was in a frame on their piano, stacked behind Wes' picture from the 2000-2001 school year. Wes' name was on the back, no address, just his name and the school year when the picture was taken.

Pretty sure that the picture came in on the tornado winds, Wald turned to the "W" section in the phone book. With only two Wegners with an "e," in Siren, he dialed the right number on the first try. "Do you have a son, Wesley?" he asked Dave. When the answer was yes, Wald told Dave he had the picture.

Dave figured Wald would like to meet the family; but with all that was happening—rebuilding his shop was at the forefront of Dave's mind—there was no time to make the trip to Cable.

One day about a month after the tornado, Wald showed up in Siren himself to hand-deliver the picture to its owners. None of the other school pictures that were on the piano have been found; and this was the only picture that made its way into Wald's driveway.

The Wegners lost 75 percent of their possessions during the tornado, which destroyed the home they built and finished six years ago, and Dave's shop, which he moved there after a fire destroyed his location on the south side of the village. No traces of their refrigerator, three love seats or a couch have been found. "I would recognize the refrigerator because of the pictures on the front," Dave commented.

What is more amazing to him is that no trace, not even parts, has been found of the solid oak staircase he had built for the house. "It was a massive set of oak stairs," he said.

Looking at pictures of the destruction on the property, including the crumbled wall of the basement where Dave and two others took shelter from the tornado, one wonders how anyone survived without injury that memorable night in June. Yet three people did.

The Wegners' daughter, Natalie, was at Wisconsin Dells that Monday. Dave, Janis and their three sons, Wes, Isaac and Josiah, went to a hockey game in Spooner. Janis left for the Dells with the boys right after the game, and Dave came back to Siren.

On the way home, he stopped at a small house that he and Siren resident Roy Ward own. The two were remodeling the house, and Roy was there with his girlfriend, Krissa, and sister, Lori. The radio was on, and Dave heard the tornado warning—a warning, not a watch.

He asked if the three wanted to go to his house. Roy and Krissa went with him; Lori headed back to town.

The television at home was on for less than a minute when the power went out. It was 8:20 P.M. Dave walked outside on a couple of occasions, looking at the sky. The phone rang. Dave answered, thinking it might be Siren Police Chief Dean Roland calling to warn them, as he had done in the past. It was one of his employees, Eric McKinley, who lives over toward Grantsburg, west of Siren. "You need to get in the basement. I saw a tornado," McKinley said.

Janis Wegner holds the picture of her son, Wesley, that was taken during the 1999–2000 school year. The picture, which was underneath the current year's photo in a frame on the Wegners' piano, was picked up by the June 18 tornado winds and deposited 80 miles away in Gilbert Wald's driveway in Cable. Shown with Janis, sitting on the edge of the basement where their house once stood, are husband, Dave, and sons, Isaac and Josiah. Photo courtesy of Inter-County Leader.

Dave hung up and walked outside. He could see low clouds streaking in from someplace. When they got to the top of the trees, he lost track of them and couldn't see where they were going. "I've never seen that before," he said. He grabbed a candle and three pillows; he, Roy and Krissa headed for the basement.

Because their property overlooks a lake, Dave had thought about where would be a safe place to go in case of high winds. His focus had zeroed in on a 5-foot by 12-foot table in the basement with a knee hole in the center and overhang on each end. "I recall telling (Roy and Krissa) we should get underneath," Dave said. Just about that time, their ears popped.

The three crawled under the table, Roy and Krissa in the knee hole and Dave on the right corner. "I don't think we were under that table even one minute," Dave said. "I heard the window blow, not just glass breaking but the huge noise of 'whoosh.' The house began to creak as the winds hit it. I never heard a train; or if there was that sound, I don't remember. I could hear the sound of wood breaking and something breaking loose."

He could see the floor joists move and the cement wall opposite them collapse into the basement. He could see daylight because the house had just disappeared. Hail as big as a fist and water were pouring into the basement. The center floor beam fell down on the table the three were under, causing the table to shift.

"I never felt scared or worried for our safety (until then)," Dave said. "I thought we were going to be trapped, with the house gone and things coming down on us. Not knowing where the house was, was unsettling."

From the time the first window blew in until the time the beam hit the table was 45 seconds.

Dave waited until the sound of air moving had stopped, then he called over to make sure Roy and Krissa were alright, before stepping on the table and shelving to crawl out of the basement. He felt awestruck, seeing things scattered all over the place when five minutes before, there had been perfect order. The sense of personal loss hadn't hit yet. It wouldn't, until about 12:30 or 1:30 A.M.

With the tornado putting him about six weeks behind in his cabinetry work, one of Dave's priorities was getting the shop back up and running. First thing the next morning, he called Brad Peterson from Peterson Construction in Webster, who brought almost his entire crew over to clean up the area and start work on a new shop.

The biggest loss in the shop was a set of tables Dave was making for the expansion of the Pour House, a Siren business that, too, was totally destroyed by the tornado. Other than that, because he had been working on an outside job, Dave didn't have a lot of projects going on in the shop.

Built just like the old shop but a bit larger, Dave and crew moved into the new Wegner Cabinetry building August 20th. The next big job is replacing the house.

Although they lost so much in personal possessions, the Wegners' mood is upbeat and positive. "It could have been worse," Janis commented. "I could have been a widow."

Editor's Note: This story reprinted with permission from the Inter-County Leader newspaper.

The Tornado's Destructive Fury

"Oh my God, everything is gone. Everything is flattened."

—*Michelle Landsberger, Tornado Survivor*

By Nancy Daniels

Michelle and Darren Landsberger lived with their two children on a small farm on the north side of Mud Hen Lake, west of Siren. The two had just about finished remodeling their house, one room at a time. They had also just finished building a new pole shed. Michelle loved living on the lake and being in a rural area, where they could raise cattle, pigs and chickens. Siren, she thought, was "smaller than Mayberry."

The day of the tornado was typical for the Landsbergers. The kids, ages five and eight, went to summer school in neighboring Grantsburg, and Darren went to work. Michelle was at home, a day off from her job as a cook/aide at Burnett County Medical Center. She was busy taking care of things around the house and yard. The kids came home from summer school around noon, played and then fed some of the Landsbergers' animals. Things were so normal.

That evening, they were all home and had just finished dinner. They were watching television, hearing reports on the bad weather. The meteorologist was talking about a storm headed for Center City in Minnesota, where Darren's parents live. They were concerned about Darren's parents, but they hadn't heard anything about the tornado heading for Siren. Still the sky was an "icky green" and it was very still. Michelle just had a "gut feeling" that something was wrong; she began collecting things like her purse, cell phone, blankets, sweatshirts and a Game Boy for the kids in case they had to head to the basement. She tried not to worry the children. That's when the power went out.

Darren looked out the window across the road to the lake and saw debris-laden water flying sideways through the air. He hollered, "Run!" Michelle and the children had just gotten into the basement, under the stairs, when a window blew out. Before Darren made it down the stairs, he saw a 30-foot pine tree ripped from the ground. Even though they were in the basement for only about a minute and a half, it seemed like an eternity. It was so loud. When the noise finally subsided, Darren went up first. Michelle and the children were so worried about his safety. They didn't know what to expect when he gave them the "all clear."

The first thing Michelle remembered seeing was the clock. It was stopped at 8:17 P.M. As she quickly glanced around, she knew their lives were changed forever. All of the work over the last ten years, shattered around them. Everything covered in broken glass and insulation. The roof and siding on the house were missing. The foundation twisted. Outside everything demolished—a shed, a partially rebuilt cattle hut, a chicken coop, a pig hut, a calf hut and most of their fencing. Their beef cattle, pigs, and chickens scattered around. One-hundred-year-old oak trees in the pasture uprooted. "Oh my God, everything is gone," Michelle thought. "Everything is flattened." Through tears, they tried to gather and find their cattle. After some time, they realized they couldn't stay in their home. So they spent the rest of the night with friends.

The next day was like a daze. It seemed hectic, not knowing where to start. They located animals far and wide, and discovered they had lost four head of cattle and four chickens. The feeder pigs had to be sold because they had nothing to keep them in. Friends and volunteers came to help cut trees and put fences back up. It was in many ways like a circus with all the people around—the power company, clean-up crews and gawkers. In the days to follow, as so many people pitched in, Michelle developed a deep appreciation for the sense of community and cooperation among her neighbors.

As it will for most everyone who experienced the storm, the twister will have a lasting impact on Michelle. She will never forget how quickly it came and how much devastation it caused to property and lives. She misses her daily routine the most. And now, whenever it gets cloudy or the wind picks up, she gets a knot in her stomach.

Coping can be difficult at times, but for the most part Michelle takes it all in stride. She's discovered how kind and supportive people can be, and how lucky she and her family are to have come out of this alive. Most of the time she's busy making "lemonade out of the lemons" this twister has handed her.

Moving On

"The past is past, and what tomorrow brings is what is high on my priority list."

—Linda Herrick, Siren Resident

By Linda Herrick

We live approximately four miles west of Siren on a hobby farm. My husband, Mike, is the manager of a manufacturing plant in Siren called North States Industries. I have been a high school teacher in Siren for the past 31 years. After a day at work we return home to do work on our farm, where we breed and raise horses and cattle. Our lives are very busy, but we enjoy our lifestyle. My brother, Greg Mravik, owns land right next to us, and can be found working alongside of us each evening. Monday, June 18, was no different.

A friend of mine, Bonnie Peterson, and I were in the neighboring town of Webster visiting another friend for most of the day, when we learned a storm was headed our direction. So we started out for home: as it would turn out directly into the path of the tornado. Mike and Greg had been planting corn in a nearby field, and were returning the planter to the neighbor when they learned bad weather was coming. When we all got home, Mike and Greg started closing the barn doors, and I said good-bye to Bonnie.

Fearing another hailstorm was coming like the one that had previously done a lot of damage to our vehicles, Mike put my PT Cruiser into the garage. As Mike, Greg and I rounded the corner to the basement door, we simultaneously looked up at the sky to the west, and were aghast to see the tornado's funnel bearing down on us. We reached for the door and hurried inside. No sooner had we positioned ourselves into a safe spot in the basement, than the "freight train" roar was upon us. As our ears popped from the pressure, we saw our personal items flying past the window. The twisting and cracking of the wood, the breaking glass and the vibration from the force of the tornado was frightening.

Then, as soon as it had come, it passed. What we heard next was the sound of hail falling on our home, which now had no roof. Stepping cautiously through the debris that was once our home and personal items was heartbreaking. Thankful that the three of us were not hurt, our concerns turned toward the animals. Walking toward the outside buildings—a pole barn, two other barns and a machinery shed—we began assessing the damage. The roofs were ripped off, and one barn had shifted from the foundation. The machinery shed, a three-sided building, now only had five supports that remained standing.

Fearing for the safety of my horses, I was calmed as we were eventually able to account for all of them. Unable to check on his cattle because of the immediate work that he had to do, Mike was sickened at the thought that they might be severely injured. This fear was compounded further, as the sounds of gunshots rang out later into the evening hours. (People were putting down badly injured animals.)

Near exhaustion, a near and dear neighbor, Ann Swenson, offered us a bed. Sleep came hard, but was welcome. Early the next morning, ready for the work that lay ahead of us, we returned to our homes. If reality had not sunk in the previous night, it was like a slap on the face as we came upon the disastrous sight of our homes. Daylight brought a more bleak picture of the destruction. Greg went to check on his trailer and saw that it had completely flipped, spewing all of his personal belongings out into the elements. We, too, were dismayed to see exactly how twisted and ripped our home was from the tornado.

A realization that set in even further as a large number of people started showing up to help with the cleanup. I wondered: "Who are all these people and where have they come from?" It still amazes me that so many volunteers came and stayed day after day to help us. Later, I thought: "How do you thank these people for all that they have done?"

Today, Greg is staying with us in what remains of our house. Mike refers to it as our "adobe." A new home is not in the near future. The barns and sheds need to be taken care of first. Life may be somewhat back to normal, but the once well-organized routine of work and then home to chores is now harder and frustrating. With no water and no electricity yet, taking care of the animals is more time consuming.

When asked what we learned about ourselves due to the tornado, I paused and responded that it has reaffirmed the knowledge that I am a "future person." The past is past, and what tomorrow brings is what is high on my priority list. Life changes all the time and you have to change with it. Mike and I worked hard for everything we had before the tornado, and we can and will work hard for everything we will have again after the tornado. That's life, and that's who Mike and Linda Herrick are.

Our People, Our Priority

"The safety of these people meant everything. The rest can be rebuilt."

—Mike Herrick, Manager of North States Industries, Inc.

By Mike Herrick

The following is a description of how I felt when I first saw early Tuesday evening (June 19) what remained of the buildings of North States Industries, Inc. Not only had the tornado the day before wreaked havoc on my own home, but it had also forced the shutdown of the place I managed, and where 71 others worked.

Despite the severe structural damage to the main plant and three warehouses, I felt an overwhelming feeling of relief and thanks. Fourteen employees were working in the plant when the tornado hit, and no one was hurt. The plant has no basement and a lot of open area on the inside. But the plant has a thousand ton press, and the employees used that as a "storm shelter." As the tornado bore down at such an amazing speed that it took many of them by surprise, the group of 14 hurried to huddle together behind the monstrous press.

After the tornado passed, they realized three semi trailers, that had been just outside the large loading dock door directly in front of the press, were pushed up to the large door and forced it up. Yet the press had stopped the trailers, fortunately preventing any harm to the frightened fourteen. The safety of these people meant everything. The rest can be rebuilt.

By Wednesday a company based in Kansas was already on site to begin rebuilding and repairing the plant. They had their work cut out for them. They had to fix the far end wall of the injection room, rebuild the main office and repair the three warehouses that had provided over 40,000 square feet of storage space. The machinery's hydraulics, electrical motors and computers also had to be cleared of debris. It was also vital to protect the machinery and finished product from further damage due to any rains. A large dehumidifying system was installed to prevent any rusting from the moisture already present. A total containment of the industrial plant was of primary concern before any rebuilding could begin in earnest.

North States Industries, Inc. was built in 1971 and for the past thirty years had grown to a manufacturer of products that are shipped both nationally and internationally. The tornado may have caused a pause in this production, but that is all it is . . . a pause.

It's Okay to Cry

"It was strange. I could see wind"

—*Russell Stewart, 81-year-old Siren Retiree*

By Luanne Swanson

Russell Stewart served in World War II, and later worked as a semi-driver. The 81-year-old traveled extensively, but through all his adventures he always called the Siren area home. Russell had spent most of his childhood in Siren. He liked the people and the friendly atmosphere.

Russell had owned his home on a lake west of Siren, for 43 years. For the first 23 years, the cabin was a weekend getaway from the Twin Cities for Russell and his family. But twenty years ago, Russell and his wife Hazle decided to make the cabin their permanent home. They remodeled and settled in there for good in 1981. (Hazle died five years ago.)

The day of the tornado was like any other Monday for Russell—laundry day. He had been in town, and on his return home was finishing up by putting away the clothes and starting supper. He was making a pork steak. After carrying clothes into the bedroom he stepped out into the middle of the dining room.

Everything seemed normal. Russell heard no hail, saw no movement of the trees across the lake. His first warning that something was wrong came very suddenly, when a window exploded. Russell turned towards the kitchen, thinking he needed to get the window there closed. As he turned, not only was the kitchen window not there, but the entire kitchen wall was missing as well. Debris was flying in all directions, crashing together. Somehow, Russell was able to remain standing.

After what seemed like an eternity, but was actually only a matter of seconds, he looked around. What was once his beautiful retirement home was now total chaos. "I need to get out of here," Russell thought. He had a hard time standing straight, which he later found out was due to the fact that his home was no longer flat on the foundation. The tornado had moved the structure and set it at an angle. When Russell finally realized what had happened, he got down and crawled for the phone. It was dead.

He looked around his surroundings and saw what appeared to be an opening to the outside. He crawled towards it and managed to escape. The whole time the structure creaked and moaned.

By this time the neighbors had come to check on him and with their help, Russell was able to make it out to the road. Someone he did not know gave him a ride. He asked to go to Tom's Bar in Siren, hoping to use a phone there to call his family. He tried calling one of his daughters, but the phone was dead. Russell began to get anxious. He wondered if his children were even alive.

Russell's daughter, Lavonne Carlson, had also been desperately searching for him. She had first gone to the school and nursing home. Not finding him, her husband suggested she head up town and stop at Tom's Bar. And there he was. She quickly assured her worried father that her family was okay, as were the families of his other two children.

The storm had hit so quickly that Russell had been unable to make it into the basement, where he normally would have gone in a storm. The next day, when he returned to his house, he felt fortunate to be alive. The whole basement was filled with cement blocks from the foundation that had given way.

Russell, who has always considered himself a strong man, learned after the tornado that a strong man can cry. In fact, he still cries when he goes back to the lake lot where his house once stood and realizes all over again that he's lost so much of what he loved.

But two months after the storm, Russell is also already the proud owner of a new home. (He was able to buy a home right after the tornado that had already been for sale before the storm.) One that he boasts has air conditioning, something he has never had before. With the mercury topping out many days this summer over 90 degrees, it's something he's thankful for. Russell is sure others will recover just fine. "You can't chase away people," he says, "who want to keep Siren home."

Home for the Holidays

"(An) unbelievable amount of help"

—*Ruth Rock, 82-year-old Siren Resident*

By Barb Lyga

Ruth Rock, an 82-year old widow, lived west of Siren on Daniel Johnson Road. Her home of 55 years held many memories. Gatherings and celebrations. Good times with family and friends. It also housed her prized possessions.

On June 18th she was sewing, with no radio or TV on throughout the day. The weather was fine. Then all at once, the power went off. She thought, however, this was not all that unusual. She called her neighbor, Gen Hunter, just to make sure she was not the only one to lose her power.

Gen replied, "Well, Ruth, don't you know there's a tornado coming? You'd better get down to the basement!" So she hung up the phone, and took eight steps. She was in front of her bathroom. That was when everything started crashing. There was a tremendous downpour; water was running down the hall from upstairs. Shattering glass came down from above. Hail the size of tennis balls and cement blocks were flying through the air.

"I could not believe that it was real—what I was seeing," Ruth said. "Too unbelievable to be real!"

Ruth watched it all from her bathroom window. The wind was twisting the trunks of trees in her yard. Trees were uprooted. She stood there for 3–4 minutes wondering: "What do I do?" Then it cleared up.

The house was a disaster. The garage was destroyed. A beam was across the car. Everything in the garage was gone, except for the chainsaw. That was untouched, in the middle of the garage. She stayed and waited that night; for the longest time, no one could get through and she could not get out.

Finally, later that evening, her daughter and son-in-law, Francine and Robert Marlow, arrived at her home. So did her two grandsons, Chet and Chad Marlow, and her granddaughter's husband, Rodney Semps. They did not sleep all night. They sat in the living room and dining room, away from all the broken glass, and talked. Happy just to be together.

When it was light, people began coming around to check on her. A Native American crew was one of the first on the scene, using their chainsaws to cut a path to Ruth's house. Another man (Ruth never found out who he was) showed up asking if she was okay. After she told him she was, he left a little tag on her mailbox. He continued down the rest of the road, doing that at each home along the way. It felt good to have so many people willing to pitch in. "Fantastic," she says, "unbelievable amount of help."

Mattresses, bedding, and other items had flown out of upstairs windows. In particular, Ruth was missing one treasured item, a quilt her mother had made. She felt bad about losing it. Thankfully, her grandson later found it near the dog pen. The beds and mattresses were gone. Ruth didn't care. She had her mother's quilt. "It was like having a piece of my life, my family back to me," Ruth said. On the porch Ruth found her antique, claw-foot table un-damaged. This, even though the porch doors and windows were gone, along with the four chairs that had been around the table. Dirt and leaves were scattered all through the house, which had shifted to the east. The floors were like a teeter-totter.

Ruth's dog had to be put to sleep because he sustained internal injuries when the kennel smashed in on him. But by some miracle, the bird in a cage in the kitchen was okay.

Ruth would later recall how surprised she had been at the speed of the storm, and how fortunate she felt to have made it through without any injuries. Had she tried to go to the basement, she likely would have blown away. (To get to there, she would have had to go outside.) The doors that covered the entrance to the basement were gone. She only had had enough time to make it to the bathroom. While many other windows in her home had blown out, the one in the bathroom did not. Through that little opening, she watched cement blocks fly by.

Ruth is currently living at a little house near her property. At her age, she says, rebuilding is a difficult task. But already the digging is done for her new home, and the septic system is in. She plans to be moved in by Christmas. "Back for the holidays," Ruth says. After 55 years on the same property, Ruth wouldn't have it any other way.

Lives Changed

"As I looked through the town at the stoplight, I truly felt sick. Before me lay the most incredible, surreal, empty scene I have ever seen."

—*Jill Glover, Siren Resident*

By Jill Glover

The daylight hours of June 18, 2001 are difficult to recall, because it turned out to be the evening hours that changed our lives and our little town so much. I know that I had been washing clothes in the laundry alcove of our tiny rented house. My husband, Joel, was still working on a farm in Grantsburg (15 miles west of Siren) around 3:00 in the afternoon, and our children and I decided to walk across our street for a quick Dairy Queen treat after we put the last load in the washer.

I had bought a horse from some friends of ours in Atlas (about 25 miles southwest of Siren), and needed to run over there and make

Photo courtesy of St. Paul Pioneer Press.

the final payment on it. Joel usually helped his dad with his farm chores after milking at the other farm. I wasn't expecting him home until after dark. So after our treat, I loaded my four-year-old son and six-year-old daughter into the car and headed out of town.

The horse was more than we hoped for. She was gentle, willing and very intelligent. The kids and I were having so much fun getting to know her and riding her that we lost track of time. By seven o'clock, my oldest, Jessica, reminded me that we hadn't eaten dinner yet. I decided that fun was fun, but we needed to eat, too. I had started to buckle Joshua, my youngest, into the car when our friends asked us to eat with them. By seven thirty, we were ready to get back to Siren.

I had homework to finish for a class I was taking in St. Paul, and the kids had had a long day. It was time to get home. We don't watch a lot of TV, and we hardly ever listen to the radio. As a former library director, I am hooked on books on tape, and listen almost exclusively to stories while I'm driving. We had also been outside for most of the afternoon and didn't notice anything strange about the weather. As we headed north through Lewis (about five miles south of Siren) on Hwy 35, I did notice the sky ahead of me getting darker and darker. I didn't think anything of it. I grew up in Siren on a little farm on Hwy 35 across the road from Little Mexico (a Mexican restaurant on the south side of town).

I remember the storm of 1976, when my two brothers and I ran from the barn to our house across the street. Trees were blowing down around us. I can still see my dad running to the house hanging on to my little sister's hand as she was flying out behind him. We've had quite

a few doozies since then, and we were usually the first to get out there afterwards and start to clear the roads. As Jess, Josh and I drove past Little Mexico that night, we noticed some tree branches and leaves blown across the road. The sky was still dark and it was about 8:25 on my watch.

We had just missed the tornado by minutes. Not knowing this yet, I drove into town in a very peaceful state of mind. Just south of Siren, my brother-in-law, Tony Dalsveen, was busy cutting up a tree that had fallen across the road by the Siren ball field. My middle school math teacher, Mike Murphy, was directing me. At that time, I was the only traffic around the mess. As I slowed down to joke with Tony, he frantically waved me away and told me to "just get outta here!" I thought he was rather rude. After all, what is the big deal? Trees fall down in storms all the time. This is Wisconsin, deal with it.

It wasn't until I got past the Pine Wood Motel, that I realized something bad had happened to Siren. The few people on the streets were looking shell-shocked, and there were electrical wires down all over the place. I don't remember seeing other vehicles on the road, it seemed like I was the only one. As I looked through the town at the stoplight, I truly felt sick. Before me lay the most incredible, surreal, empty scene I have ever seen.

In the gray light, I remember looking through Siren and being able to see Crooked Lake Park (on the north end of town) from the stoplight. There was nothing in my field of vision to hinder my sight. I was almost physically ill. My daughter started screaming hysterically at this point, and my son started crying. I don't ever remember being scared in the beginning. I knew where my children were and I thought I knew where my husband was.

He never comes home before dark. I knew he was safe at his parents' house in Grantsburg. I knew he would be worried about us though. For some strange reason, I thought if I could get home and call him, it would be ok. I remember seeing the cars overturned and blown into the Pour House (a restaurant and bar on the north end of town); the pharmacy's roof had blown off, the windows and entryway totally gone. There wasn't a lot left of Russ' Old Fashioned Meats. I remember thinking that I hadn't picked up any steaks for our grill out Thursday, and now I wouldn't be able to. I guess I thought I'd deal with it when I got home.

It was my daughter who first noticed that we didn't even have a home anymore. I don't know why I thought it would still be there, but I did. We looked across the parking lot of the Main Street Market and couldn't see the roof of our house through the heaping mass of fallen trees. Every power line on the street was, literally, on the street. I think it was at that moment, that I knew what Tony meant. With Jess and Joshua screaming in the back, I knew Siren was not where I wanted to be. As I turned around at the Main Street Market, I spotted my Dad running past the Pour House with a couple of tanks of oxygen. I yelled that the kids and I were safe, Joel was out of town and the house, as far as I could tell, was gone.

Then we headed back to the south of town to my parent's house to make some phone calls. First I wanted to call Joel. Then, I wanted to call the nursing home. I work at Capeside Cove nursing home part time, and wanted to make sure everyone there was ok. I knew my Mom would have been called in to help there and I wanted her to know we were all right too.

It was after 10:00 by the time I got through to my mother-in-law. When she informed me that Joel was not at her house, but rather at the house in Siren, I think my heart stopped. I knew there wasn't a house there. My mother-in-law assured me that Joel was fine. She didn't know where he was right at that moment. But she had called him just after the tornado hit and he had said that he was okay. I was just anxious to see for myself. I didn't know how to get a message to anyone in town. I knew I couldn't get back into town. Just outside my parents' house on Highway 35 there was a stopped line of traffic that went back probably close to three miles. Most were being turned around at Little Mexico and re-routed around the town. A few people were getting in, but it was a long wait to get to the head of the line.

So I waited there at my neighbor's house with our friend from across the street and my children, hoping to hear some news from inside Siren. We were less than one mile out of town, but we were learning what was happening from hourly calls from my friend in Minneapolis. We had no electricity, TV, or radio. We couldn't phone anyone in Siren either. Finally, my mom and dad came home around 1:00.

Joel came through the door around 1:30. Despite the excitement, it was the quietest I've ever seen him. He wasn't tired, and he wasn't going to be able to sleep for a long time. But his eyes were bleak, his movements were slow and his soul was very, very still. He didn't say a word as he held onto me, but I could tell that he was very shaken. With the exception of his face, his whole body was plastered with insulation, tree leaves and debris. As he went down to the lake to bathe, he told me what happened.

He had gotten done at his dad's farm early, and decided to go home. He was just going to take a shower when the electricity went out. We're not used to living in town, so when the electricity goes out we generally assume there's no water either. So Joel decided to lie down for a little nap. He usually gets up at 4:00 A.M., so by 8:00 P.M., he's pretty tired. Almost immediately after laying down, he heard the rain start. He got up to close the window in the kids' room, and as he crossed the living room, the wind picked up.

In five seconds the wind went from non-existent, to strong enough to blow down an oak tree two feet in diameter with no resistance from the tree whatsoever. It took Joel five more seconds to get across the living room, into the bedroom and into the closet. He had just hit the closet, when the ceiling came down, the roof blew off and the walls blew out. He hid in the closet another two or three minutes, then stuck his head out. He was hit immediately by hail. As he was coming out of the closet (in his underwear I might add) the telephone started ringing.

He walked out of the half of house that was blown away, into the half that still had the telephone on the counter. The caller was his friend from Danbury (15 miles north of Siren) warning him to get out of the house. Apparently, there was a big tornado coming directly towards Siren. Joel told her that he was now well aware of that, but thanked her anyway for the warning. He told her that he was standing in half of our house. The strangeness in his voice told her he wasn't joking. He found a pair of jeans in the dryer of the laundry room, and proceeded to climb his way out of the house.

A tree had landed on his truck, and wires were down everywhere. After a while, rescue workers came by and told him to go to the Main Street Market to be counted. Then, he joined a crew of men, helping clear the streets and getting the trees away from people's doors so they could get out. The gas and the water lines had ruptured, so the working conditions were dangerous. Somewhere along the way, he ran into my dad, who told him that we were all okay. About 1:00 A.M., he ran into a friend, who helped him cut the tree off his truck and get out.

He was then able to get on the street and get his first real glimpse of the town. It was beyond shocking. It looked like Siren had been bombed. You see pictures like that on the news, but you rarely have anything to compare them to, and so you can't fully comprehend the massive, sickening destruction. He knew what Siren looked like before. And now, he knew what it looked like after.

Over and over in the days to come, we would hear, "I can't even recognize the streets anymore." We would see aerial pictures of Siren and not be able to locate one single landmark. A house three doors down from us was ripped totally from its foundation and flung a quarter mile backward (to the west), coming to a rest on Old 35. I don't think they ever did find the Dairy Queen freezer. People found records from the Siren Dental Clinic in Spooner (more than 25 miles east of Siren). The sign from the Auto Stop was found in Trego (more than 30 miles northeast of Siren). Everybody knows what happened to the hockey arena. And the same thing happened to the Blue Collar Auto Body.

(They were flattened.) But the four churches remained unharmed as well as the school and, thankfully, the nursing home.

In the next few hours, these remaining sanctuaries would fill with the homeless and flood of emergency workers and volunteers. Donations of money, equipment, food and supplies would flow profusely into Siren. It took me two full days after the tornado to figure out just how to start cleaning up. It would have taken longer, if the volunteers hadn't just started shoveling things out. It took Jessica and Joshua three full days before they recognized the place. They wanted to go home, not realizing that they were already at their house. They lost some of their things. But the most important thing, we didn't lose each other.

I truly feel angels guarded the whole town that night. Everybody has a story about why they were not where they were supposed to be that night. Why was the meeting at the hockey arena cancelled? Why did the people in the Auto Stop move to the other bathroom? How did numerous people just happen to glance to the west, just as the tornado dropped out of the sky? This is just one family's account of that night. Most everyone will have a similar, yet different story.

But no matter whom you talk to, everyone will agree: A spirit of love and benevolence swept into our town as the tornado swept out. And we will never be the same.

Editor's Note: Jill Glover submitted this story from a journal entry she wrote shortly after the tornado.

Escape from Death

"So this is what dying feels like. Don't worry. Don't fight it and it will be quick and painless."

—*Mary Peterson, Siren Resident*

By Mary Peterson

Monday, June 18, 2001 started out very uneventful. I went to work at North States Industries, a manufacturing plant. My husband, Brian, was at his job at Capeside Cove nursing home. Our son, Richard, did the typical kid stuff. If I recall correctly, the day was a little warm, but nothing unusual.

In the evening, Richard and the other boys from the varsity baseball team went with the coaching staff to Grantsburg (15 miles west of Siren) to play their weekly game. I remember hearing severe storm warnings on the television around 7:30 P.M. I was busy listening to that while watching out the west window, waiting for the boys to get back from their game. A little after 8:00, I was getting ready to leave for the school to pick up Richard, figuring he should be getting back by then. I no sooner thought about leaving, when I heard Richard come walking in. He told us they had called off the game because of lightning.

Brian jokingly told us he needed some ice cream. Okay, I thought, Richard and I would go to town. That way, we could also check out the new videos at Auto Stop, a convenience store in Siren. We didn't worry too much about the storm. I mean, for weeks we had heard storm warnings, but they had always missed us and gone elsewhere. So we headed off to town. We had just gotten to Siren's only stoplight, when the electricity went out. I decided to stop at Capeside Cove, where Brian worked, to see how they were. Everything was fine.

From there, Richard and I continued on toward Yourchuck's, a store in Siren where you can buy just about anything. We were just passing The Lodge, a hotel on the north end of town, when we both looked west at the swirling clouds. Well, no big deal, but it looked like we were going to get a storm after all. We decided to stop at Auto Stop, just in case it started to hail. A year ago I had lost a car to hail, while it was parked outside at home. I didn't want that to happen again. We figured the canopy would protect this vehicle.

We were getting out of the car, when we heard Cory Sederlund, the store's manager, hollering for us to get inside and go to the men's restroom. Richard and I both ran behind Cory and a customer. I had to hurry Richard up a little bit because he wanted to call his dad first to let him know we were heading for cover. I had to tell him that everything would be okay, and that Brian would trust us to care for ourselves. Then we heard someone else holler that his ears were "popping." Hmm, I thought, mine were too. Okay, so maybe the severe thunderstorm was coming our way after all. All eight of us huddled in the men's room. I was really embarrassed when I let out a little scream when part of the ceiling tile came down. I really felt stupid and apologized. I did not want to be remembered as a scared woman.

Then we started to hear some banging or something. I recall a strange, but strong urge to go to the women's restroom. Later, Richard reminded me I had yelled out that we should go there. I recall reaching the doorknob of that room, but never realizing how severe things really were. Well, all eight of us made it into the room and some of us huddled together on our knees on the floor. Richard told me later that I automatically put my arms around the people near me, as did Cory, who was protecting his employees.

Then, I had a very strange sensation. I felt alone, apart from everyone else, and not in the room with the others. I felt cushioned and protected. I remember thinking, "So this is what dying feels like." Then a calm feeling came over me, as did an inner peace. "Don't worry," I thought, "don't fight it and it will be quick and painless." I didn't have a worry, or a thought about anyone or anything else, and then I was back in the room with the others. I recall the sensation of the building shaking and then the roof going and the ceiling tile falling, as the softball-sized hail fell from the sky. I really felt relief, when it went quiet for a few moments. I

blurted out, "Well, do you think it will be okay to look out from under this protection to see the sky?" Richard hollered back, "Oh mom, we are in the eye." Okay, I thought, so I waited. Then I looked. It was finally all over.

I recall all of us leaving that little room. There was no roof, but we did have the four walls of the room intact. I also recall walking through the debris-filled floor. Then I heard Siren Police Chief Dean Roland's voice, "Is anyone in there? Is anyone hurt?" We replied that we were okay. When I asked if there was anything I could do, Dean was already gone, checking on others in the town.

Because Richard was worried his dad would be fretting about us, a woman who was with us during the ordeal handed him her cell phone. Richard could only blurt out to his dad that we were both okay. He had to quickly hang up after that because we had to head for cover again. So we returned to the room. We were not there for long, when we realized that all was finally over.

After we left the bathroom for the second time, I stopped to talk to a friend in his vehicle. I told him, and the others there, that Richard and I had to get to Capeside Cove, the nursing home in Siren. So the two of us started walking. The people in town were in total shock. I guess that was to be expected because it did take us all by surprise. There had been so many false alarms before. This was now the real thing. As we walked toward the nursing home, Richard and I would stop to give people hugs and talk to them, letting them know we were okay.

I kept thinking how there were wires down, but thank God they were not live wires. He had provided protection by taking out the electricity. We were really blessed and protected. We were so thankful to be alive, that as we approached some people on Main Street, Richard asked if we were still going to have the Fourth of July celebration. People looked at us startled that we would even think of something like that after what had happened. They did not know how close to death we had been.

When we got to Capeside, we realized the nursing home had not been hit. They had a few broken windows, but the residents there were okay. I was relieved, and knew we had to find Brian. So we headed for Main Street. As we approached the downtown, we saw Brian arriving into town. Richard and I stopped as Brian got out of the truck, and we had a group hug.

I found out later that, after we had left for town, the tornado was approaching Siren. Brian had heard about it, but he had no way of contacting us. So he sat in awe as a dark cloud approached from the west. He left the west window in the dining room when he saw the swamp grass go flat. He ran to the east side of the house, in time to see the truck being jostled around by the wind. Then he heard the tinkling of glass as the west window blew out.

When the storm seemed to have passed over him, Brian went into town. He doesn't really remember how he got into town, he just knew that he had to do it. On the way home after meeting us, he saw all the downed trees he had circumvented. How he was able to get around all of them was a small miracle. He later told us that until Richard had called him, he had felt that we had been taken from him.

We were among some of the lucky people. We had some roof and siding damage, and lost some trees. I found out the following morning, we had also lost my car. Right after the storm, I had noticed some missing windows, but had not known that I had a flat tire and a broken tie rod. I didn't realize until weeks later that the tornado had ripped out the station's gas pumps. But we didn't have one fire or explosion. We were very blessed.

Eye of the Storm

> "People's dreams, realities, their livelihoods, were all crushed in the blink of an eye. That pain is the kind that pulls and tugs at your heartstrings."
>
> —*Kent Boyer, Siren Dairy Queen Owner*

By Amy Swanson

After months of hard work Kara Alden and Kent Boyer opened their new Dairy Queen on the north end of Siren on April 2, 2001. The previous fall they had torn down their old drive-in, The Fancy Freeze, to make way for the new restaurant. It had been a lot of hard work, but they were finally harvesting the fruits of their labor. There was still a little bit of work to do here and there. But the brother and sister team had gotten the store open in time for the busy summer season.

Kent, a single man living in Frederic 10 miles south of Frederic, had come to really like the Siren community. People in Siren seemed to care a great deal for one another. And they were very supportive, Kent thought, after he and Kara opened their new business. Kara thought about the same thing. She enjoyed the positive, friendly attitudes and the way residents really worked to make things happen. Kara and her husband Donald's home was just three and a half miles south of Siren, an area she called her "up north paradise."

The day of the storm, a Monday, Kara and Kent were at their Dairy Queen store trying to recover from the weekend. It had been a good two days—both for business and weather. The brother and sister were working along with seven employees to clean and decorate cakes to re-stock the freezer. It was a hot and muggy day, but no matter. Inside it was nice and air-conditioned.

Later that evening, after the power went out, the employees began reimbursing all the customers. Without power, they could no longer serve anyone. During this time, Kent and Kara's mother, Lavonne, as well as their brother, Dale, had called to warn them of the approaching storm. But they were both cut short during the phone call because Kent and Kara were so busy with the customers. After everyone had been reimbursed, Kara and the other employees started their evening cleaning, and planned on leaving about an hour early for the night. Kent went to the back of the store to check the weather. As it began to get really windy and start hailing, Kent picked up a piece of the hail and brought it to the front of the store to show the others. By the time he got there, the windows started breaking and the garbage cans were tipping over.

Kara told everyone—the seven employees and a friend of Kara's who had stopped due to the weather—to get into the walk-in cooler, which was centrally located in the building. As they had made their way back to the cooler, Kent was holding the door, and had to come around the door to get into the cooler. By this time, debris was flying and falling everywhere. Kent crouched down with one hand covering his head, and the other holding tightly onto the cooler door. The cooler was located next to a hallway, and Kent described it like being in a wind tunnel. The pressure was very evident and the force of the wind whipping through the building was strong.

Inside the cooler, Kara, her friend, and the seven employees were all holding each other and praying. They were all quite afraid, especially Kara after she learned her brother wasn't in the cooler. "Oh my God," she thought, "Kent didn't make it in." Big tears rolled down her face.

Then the wind seemed that it was calming down, and Kent began thinking of the things they were going to have to clean up; just "minor damage" he thought to himself. But then another burst of wind came through and he could feel it passing through the building.

From Kent's position he could see the door to the walk-in freezer, and when that second wind came hurling through, it lifted the walk-in freezer up off the slab. After the tornado had torn the freezer free, the back door burst open and the wind was so loud that Kent couldn't hear any of the things breaking and being tossed about.

About 45 seconds later, all of the damage had been done. No one inside the Dairy Queen was hurt during the storm. Kent walked back to the parking lot to check on the vehicles; they were all destroyed. Joel Glover, a resident of First Avenue just behind the Dairy Queen, came walking toward Kent. Joel had been home alone and had sat inside a closet in the center of his house. Joel looked as if he had just been tarred and feathered, Kent thought. Insulation and dirt was all over him from the storm.

As they looked around after the storm, all Kent and Kara could see around them was total devastation. Their parents had been at their home in Frederic during the storm, and now decided to drive up to see if the kids were all right. But as the made their way up Highway 35, LaVonne and John Boyer had to stop because of trees and power lines on the road. Retired Siren teacher Mike Murphy had been cutting trees off of the road, and told the Boyers what route they could use instead to get to the Dairy Queen. The Boyers pushed on. Nothing was going to stop them from getting to their children.

Once they finally arrived at the Dairy Queen, they were overjoyed to learn that their children, and all of the employees, had escaped unharmed. A few minutes later, they set themselves to the task of starting the clean up. First, LaVonne and Kara took the cakes they had decorated that day to the school and to the Methodist church. Kent was inside speaking with people from the Twin Cities media, who had called the Dairy Queen to ask about the storm. The Boyer family drove their employees home because their vehicles were destroyed.

After their insurance company determined the building had to be torn down, Kent and Kara, along with help of numerous volunteers, finished cleaning up and getting equipment

The Siren Dairy Queen, owned by members of the Boyer family, opened April 2, a little more than two months before the tornado hit town. While Kent Boyer, his sister Kara Alden and their employees and customers in the building escaped injury, the new building had to be taken down and rebuilt. Photo courtesy of Inter-County Leader.

out of the building. In those days after the storm, Kent thought the town seemed like the busiest place on earth because of all the people that had come to help or see the damage. "People's dreams, realities, their livelihoods, were all crushed in the blink of an eye," Kent says. "That pain is the kind that pulls and tugs at your heartstrings."

Later, Kara reflected on how lucky she felt to have been in that new building when the storm hit: "The Fancy Freeze would never had made it through that storm, and down with it could have went the lives of my employees and/or myself. I am so thankful that Kent and I had built the Dairy Queen. And the thought of having to rebuild and start over is nothing compared to the thought of having been in the Fancy Freeze while this all happened. Thank God!"

So Much Lost

"It may have been at that moment, when I thought we might not live through this."

—*Rita Gjonnes, Siren Resident*

By Rita Gjonnes

Siren resident Rita Gjonnes has been in real estate for 15 years. In 1997 she purchased a RE/MAX franchise, and opened RE/MAX Northwoods on the village's main thoroughfare Highway 35/70. A rather simple but completely remodeled, cedar-sided building on a corner lot surrounded by an assortment of native pines, tall oaks and a few birch trees.

A couple of years later, Rita purchased the house next door for future expansion. Rita's mother, Helen Gilfillan, resided with Rita and her 15-year-old son, Kyle Gjonnes. Rita and her family had, in fact, just moved into the house next to the office and were remodeling it—adding a 3rd bedroom and expanding the bathroom and kitchen. Rita's brother, Jim Gilfillan, and his wife, Nancy Gilfillan, had recently sold their home in Arizona, moving to Siren to be closer to family members.

As Rita recalls it, the day of the tornado was sunny, kind of humid but comfortable. About half an hour before the storm, Rita was sitting in her office alone drafting a purchase offer, when she noticed the clouds moving in. "I knew my mother would be tracking the storm," Rita said, "so I popped over to the house to watch the weather. It pretty much looked like it was heading north of us closer to the Pine City/ Hinckley area." (Two communities on the Minnesota side of the Wisconsin/Minnesota border.) The phone rang and it was Rita's brother, Jim, saying he was concerned about the approaching storm. Jim and Nancy lived in a mobile home.

Rita told him to gather up his wife and dog (Snickers), and come over to her house, where it would be safer. Still not expecting much more than a thunderstorm Rita and Jim walked over to the RE/MAX office to take down the new flags he had mounted on the building only a few days earlier. As they tried to remove the poles from their holders the wind made it increasingly difficult to handle the 3 x 5 pieces of flapping nylon. Finally, they were able to wind up the flags, carefully placing them in the corner just inside the door of the office. They then returned to the house.

By this time the lightning was fast and furious. The kind that makes you break out in goose bumps, or flinch in anticipation of that loud crack of thunder that usually follows. But Rita started to realize that they had only heard a couple, maybe three big claps of thunder. The sound then basically just turned into one big continuous rumble. "Little did I know that it was not thunder at all," Rita said. "The bowling ball rumble I heard was probably that of the tornado passing over Penta Hill." (Penta Hill is an area just West of Siren.)

To the west it was very dark. But to the east the sky was still blue with fluffy cumulous clouds. The wind was getting stronger and stronger. Watching out the back door, Rita saw a man on a bike pulling a small child appear and then just as quickly disappear. As trash can covers, large branches with green leaves, paper and other debris started flying past her open door, she feared for the man with the child. Just at that moment Siren Police Chief Dean Roland drove past screaming over a bullhorn, "TOUCH DOWN IN GRANTSBURG!" Grantsburg, Rita thought, they still had time.

But one look in the sky, seeing those puffy white clouds moving at record speed toward that huge ugly black mass in the west, she realized they were in serious trouble. The wind became very cold. Rita turned to Jim and said, "This is like nothing I have ever seen." He asked where they should go, and the only thing Rita knew for sure was to get to the innermost part of the house.

They quickly closed all the windows and doors. The four of them, along with the two dogs, crouched down on the floor at the end of the narrow hall leading to the bedrooms. (Rita's son, Kyle, was in Frederic, 10 miles south of Siren, with his dad.) The wind continued to pick up speed as it hurled debris against the house and roof with tremendous force and loud dead thuds. First it was small parts of trees, perhaps garbage cans, then mail boxes, grocery carts, washing machines, stoves, 200-pound desks, then cars, trucks and entire walls of buildings. Rita kept thinking, "When will it stop?"

As the four of them huddled in the corner, their eyes would meet, and an entire conversation would take place without a spoken word. Just then all of the windows starting blowing out, one after the other. They were peppered with shattered glass. "It may have been at that moment, when I thought we might not live through this," Rita would later recall. Once the windows were out, it was like a vacuum, sucking oxygen, plugging our ears. And yet at the same time, it felt like the house had filled with helium as it started lifting from the foundation. Rita's brother looked at her and said, "The house is lifting up. Here we go." Rita started to pray "God, please let it stop!"

It eventually wound down; it seemed to Rita as if she hadn't taken a breath through the whole thing. She stood up, trying to steady her legs. Jim looked up at her and said, "Rita, we are in the eye, there will be more." Well, there was more, but nothing like the leading edge of that terrible monster. By comparison the second half was like the fine mist of the rinse cycle in a car wash. When they were certain it was over, they got up and started looking out the holes that once contained glass. No one was prepared for what they saw.

The first place Rita looked was out the door to the backyard. "Gone! Everything is gone," Rita said. "Mom, look, look, mom, RE/MAX is gone! I think RE/MAX is gone." She kept repeating it over and over again. She just couldn't get past the word gone. Everything was gone.

All that remained of RE/MAX was the bathroom sitting atop the slab. Rita heard a hissing and could smell a heavy odor from broken gas lines. An eerie stillness and silence hung over the entire village. No cars or electric motors running. No movement. It was like when the power goes off in your house, and everything gets quiet. You could have heard a pin drop. They meandered their way through the debris to the front door. Rita was overwhelmed by the strong scent of pine from fallen trees. She could hear dripping water, almost as if every drop was amplified by a slow motion echo, similar to water dripping inside a cave.

Rita's next thought was the people: "Oh my God, people have to be dead. Who? How many? I just knew people, a lot of people, had to be dead. Where do we begin? What to do next? I need to help somebody; no someone needs to help me. Where is everybody?" As all of these questions were running through Rita's mind, people started coming from everywhere gathering in the Pour House parking lot. (The Pour House is a restaurant and bar right next door to Rita's home and office.) The village started to come alive again, first with the soft mumbling of disoriented, confused people, and soon after that, the sounds and activities of emergency equipment—fire trucks, ambulances, police cars, gas and electric trucks. In the distance, they could also hear chainsaws buzzing and hammers pounding.

The next day, every single RE/MAX agent managed to make it to the shattered office, wearing their orange admission bracelet that allowed them to get past security. Tuesdays they normally had a weekly office meeting and tour. This day, they showed up for a very different reason, simply to offer what help they could. Initially, they shared their grief through hugs, kisses and tears. They, too, had lost much. After the shock wave began to pass, one by one they started poking through the rubble. It was a pathetic sight. "I have never felt such a tremendous sadness and feeling of complete helplessness," Rita said, "as they searched for something familiar."

As time went on laughter replaced the tears. The mood was changing. Rita heard conversations inspired by a piece of broken or twisted metal, a picture or perhaps a piece of paper with some writing on it. Someone would shout, "Hey, do you guys remember when we put this note on Mike's car?" Each agent had a little pile, neatly stacked and isolated one from the others. From this came an important life lesson for Rita: Things of material value can be reduced to rubble, but shared memories last forever.

The media were ever present doing their job, asking questions about what happened. But it was impossible for Rita to share thoughts and feelings not yet known to her. She had not lived it yet. There was no end to the story in sight. It was only chapter one of many chapters to come. The days passed as if everything was happening in slow motion. A feeling of bewilderment and confusion swept over Rita as she tried to sort out what needed to be done. All of the volunteers helped her get through these difficult moments. They were wonderful and caring. They gave her hope. Many of them were just as awestruck as she was. Friendships developed during the coming days as everyone pitched in to help. Friendships Rita hopes will last.

Within a few days of the tornado Rita and other agents needed to set up a temporary office somewhere. They had a meeting to discuss their options. The owners of Heart of the North Homes, Doug Quenzer, Al Glorvigen and Rick Harder, invited the RE/MAX folks to join them in their office about a mile north of Siren on Highway 70. The Siren Telephone Company had them up and running at the new location within days.

Many things were happening in a very short amount of time. RE/MAX agents and staff worked day and night—painting, building and posting signs for our new location; cleaning up and moving debris; making numerous trips for supplies and equipment; bringing in tables, chairs, printers and faxes from their homes; and restoring files with real estate listings. They even conducted a closing two days after the tornado.

RE/MAX offices from across the country sent cards, letters, equipment and funds. Regional managers from Bloomington, Minnesota, and Milwaukee, Wisconsin, actually came to help clean up.

Although the tornado took her office, home, car, snowmobiles, garage and personal belongings, Rita has gained much more than could ever be taken. She is in the process of building a new home and office building, and friends and family have helped her rebuild her life.

Today, Rita misses the trees, having points of reference in town, and most of all she misses not having time to spend with her best friend, Julie Young. Buried in a pile of appointments and exasperating paperwork, life has changed, and time is limited at least for the moment. Rita uses a technique she's developed over the last 20 years to deal with life's calamities. She calls it her "scale of life." Everything that happens to Rita must fit on the scale, which goes from one to ten. Although she has never had a ten, she has had some eights, which she considers pretty normal at the age of 50. The night of the tornado was a seven. During the days that followed—as Rita learned so many people had escaped death or injury, and folks began putting their lives back together—that seven changed to a six.

Rita firmly believes the town will come back better and stronger than ever—not because of the new buildings or trees, but because of the people who live in Siren.

Looking Forward

"I continue to be in awe of what has happened, but also what continues to happen. Siren will be back."

—*Karen Howe, Siren Resident*

By Nancy Daniels

A dream came true in May of 2000 for Jeff and Karen Howe. That was the month the Siren residents had their grand opening for The Shops at the Lodge. The building, built by Jeff, housed Studio Works, Sentiments by Hannah Mae, The Chattering Squirrel Coffee Shop and Karen and Jeff's own business, Syren General Store. Siren was having a growth spurt. Tourism had increased, with shoppers looking for gifts and mementoes from the "North Woods." Business had been good for the Howes, and they were anticipating another good year with the start of the summer season.

All of that changed the night of June 18, 2001. Ball games were cancelled because of the predicted thunderstorms, so the Howes were at their home on the north shore of Crooked Lake. Their girls, Lauren, 11, and Sarah, 8, had been sent to the basement to "play", so they wouldn't worry about the storm warnings.

Jeff and Karen began videotaping what they were seeing; dark clouds, large hail and wind. They did not realize that the tornado was going through just south of them, around the point in Crooked Lake. Up until the time the power went out, they had been watching the storm warnings on Channel 5 and Burnett County was no longer flashing, so they assumed that the tornado had not touched down.

Jeff called to check on his brother, John. Minutes into the conversation, John saw the tornado and jumped into his small storm cellar. He did not realize it had taken half of his house away.

As soon as Jeff had gotten off the phone with John, he received a phone call from Jim Richison, the manager of The Lodge at Crooked Lake, a hotel on the north end of town. He called to let them know that the front of their store was damaged. Jeff went into Siren immediately and called Karen to come in because the store was "really damaged!" It was difficult to assess the full extent of the destruction that evening, but they could tell that even though it was still standing, the building had been moved by the tornado. They spent the rest of that evening securing the store, calling family and friends to let them know they were safe and getting very little sleep.

In the daylight, things looked even worse.

The pure strength of the storm became evident, when they saw that the west end of their 50-by-130-foot building had been moved 22 feet to the south! The anchor bolts were completely sheared off. That end of the building was home to Studio Works, a stained glass gift shop. Even though the building had shifted that far, many of the windows and floor displays looked as though they had not been touched. The east end, where the Howe's business, the Syren General Store, was located, moved four feet to the south. The tornado took the 50-foot porch, and it was never found. When the porch left, the east wall came down, exposing the contents of their store.

The damage was devastating to say the least, but the response of their friends, and people they didn't even know, was overwhelming. Karen said, "We will forever be grateful for the people who came to help or just to give us a hug. Without their help it would have been unbearable. Just knowing that so many people cared, gave us the strength and will to move ahead."

And moving ahead is just what they are doing. They are already rebuilding and making little changes and improvements on the original plan. They are staying busy, dreaming about the possibilities for the future, staying involved in the volunteer efforts and taking breaks when they need to. Through it all, they've learned that they can cope in the face of disaster, especially with the help of so many wonderful people.

"I will never forget what it felt like seeing Siren after the tornado or the efforts to clean up," Karen said. "I will never forget how thankful I felt knowing my friends and family were safe. I will never forget seeing how powerful nature can be. I continue to be in awe of what has happened, but also what continues to happen. Siren will be back. The sign and the shirts that were made after the storm said a lot: 'THANK GOD WE'RE ALIVE!' And I thank God for the opportunities that continue to become evident each day."

Open just a year, The Shops at The Lodge complex owned by Jeff and Karen Howe was left in shambles after the tornado hit. The building had to be taken down to the concrete slab and completely rebuilt. This aerial photograph was taken by DNR pilot Joe Sprenger.

Perseverance

"We'll Be Back. But Better"

—Sign in front of Russ' Old Fashioned Meats after tornado

By Amy Swanson

Russ and Terri Erickson had just opened their meat shop in Siren two months before the tornado. It had been a dream of theirs for a long time, and it finally had come true. Business was good. The shop was busy. In fact, shortly after they opened, they realized they would probably need to add on. They both enjoyed owning a business in a small town like Siren. People they knew were always stopping by to visit.

The day of the storm, Russ and Terri were working at their shop, Russ' Old Fashioned Meats, located right on Highway 35/70 running through the middle of town. They had cleaned up earlier than usual, otherwise they would have been at the shop when the storm hit. Instead, the two had closed early, then went to Webster and were back at their home on the south side of town. One of their daughters had warned them of a possible tornado, but they didn't see anything on the television so they ignored the warning. Russ' father soon called and told Russ and his family to get to his house; Russ and Terri's house doesn't have a basement. On the way to Russ' parents' house, they actually drove through the storm.

Ten minutes after it was over, Russ and Terri first saw the destruction at their business. For the rest of the night, they spent time setting up generators and security lights to prevent looting. At 4:30 the next morning Russ, Terri, and many other volunteers, began cleaning up. Outside of their shop they set up a huge grill so they could grill steak and other food for the volunteers. Their friend, Ted Ricci, bought $200.00 worth of meat to give away in front of the store, doing the grilling himself. (Ted felt the least he could do to help out Terri and Russ was feed the people who were volunteering in the clean-up efforts at the store.) Terri and Russ also brought meat from home to give away because the meat from the store was no good. People donated every day to keep the grilling going. For a week Holiday gas station donated meat and buns, ice and pop.

Russ was also one of the first business owners to paint a message to community members on the particleboard covering up the broken windows. His read, "We'll Be Back. But Better."

Russ and Terri were amazed by all the volunteers who pitched in. There were many whose names they never even learned. One day while they were cleaning up, one of their friends, Karolyn Kroll, got pinned by the forklift. She dislocated her hip and had to go to the hospital. She came back later that night to apologize for not being able to finish out the day helping.

Since the storm, Russ and Terri have gone from working 80 hours a week to zero. Day by day, though, things are getting better. But it is especially hard, they say, dealing with insurance companies. And they are saddened that all the trees are gone. Every time it storms, a nervous feeling swells up inside of them. They know what storms can do.

As far as their business is concerned, Russ and Terri felt a month after opening that the building needed to be enlarged. So for them, the silver lining of the storm was that they could rebuild and, as they promised right after the storm, be "bigger and better." At the end of August, just before the Labor Day Weekend, Russ and Terri did just that, reopening their enlarged store.

The Message

"Sorry, because of the tornado we can't be at the phone. Jackie's looking for her paddleboat, and Larry's looking for his washers and dryers. We will get back to you when we find them."

—Message on Myrmels' Answering Machine

By Jackie Myrmel

I was at home with my husband, Larry, the night of the storm, and first heard a tornado warning for Burnett County on TV around 8:00 P.M. About 15 minutes later, the power went off. At 8:25, Larry went outside to listen to the radio in his truck. On the radio station he was listening to, they said there was a tornado warning for the area effective until 8:30. He came in the house and said the tornado warning was just about over. (The Myrmels live on Doctor's Lake, which is to the west of town on the outskirts of Siren.)

We looked out our patio door and could see a funnel coming across the lake, and we could hear a sound like a train coming. We decided we had better go in the walk-in closet in the bedroom. It lasted only about 15 seconds. We heard all kinds of scary sounds. Glass breaking. Boards ripping. The sound of a freight train. We thought: "We are going to be sucked out of our house and go flying off like Mary Poppins." I could not breathe. It was like the tornado had sucked the air out of me.

Then Larry opened the closet door and could see the sky above. What an awful feeling that was. As we looked around, we realized that was the only undamaged part of the house. The outside walls were still there, but the tornado had sucked out the insides of the house. The garage was also wrecked.

Larry wanted to get to the laundromat we own in town. We worried about whether someone had been in there during the tornado. What if they were trapped or injured? But Larry couldn't use the truck in the yard to get to town. It had a tree on top of it, and was all banged up. He tried to walk to the laundromat and get our other truck, but realized he couldn't make it there and back before dark.

So he returned, got me and we went through the jungle for about 30 minutes along Old 35 (a road on the west side of the village). Trees were crisscrossing all the roads. Power lines were down everywhere. We crawled around them, trying to avoid danger. Thankfully, we had flashlights to help guide us. We finally found a ride to the Pine Wood Motel on the south side of town.

Larry was still bound and determined to get to the laundromat, no matter what. When we finally did at 1:30 A.M, we saw that it was heavily damaged. But our worst fears were put to rest: No one had been hurt or trapped in the building.

We started cleaning up right away the next day. It was hard to know where to start. Thankfully, our son, Jeff, came with his bobcat and splitter. His friends and our granddaughter also pitched in and helped us, as did many friends. Two couples, Steve and Debbie Hauklind and Bill and Sherrie Mavves, worked with us for about 4 days. Without their help, and that of all the other volunteers, we could never have gotten things cleaned up.

We were also fortunate to have people give us a place to live for two months. First we stayed at a very nice cabin on the Clam River owned by Mike and Marilee Ryan from Alaska, formerly from Grantsburg, Wisconsin. Then we moved to a condo by the Yellow Lake Lodge, owned by Dennis and Nancy Bursh. Thank you. We will never forget how much you helped us.

Now, two months after the storm, we are happy to say our home and laundromat are about 80% fixed. We hope to have both places completely fixed by the middle of October.

Throughout it all, we have managed to maintain a sense of humor. The message for a long time on our phone was: "Sorry, because of the tornado we can't be at the phone. Jackie's looking for her paddleboat, and Larry's looking for his washers and dryers. We will get back to you when we find them."

One Minute of Terror

"It was hard for me to believe that everybody had walked away, basically without a scratch."

—Greg Hunter, Pour House Supper Club Owner

By Jill Gloodt, Nancy Daniels and Chad Thomas

After finishing work, Clark Jewell went home to switch vehicles. The auto mechanic had been driving his restored 57 Chevy, but had decided to take his 88 Olds instead that night. He was headed into Siren for a burger and beer at the Pour House Supper Club. Clark, like many Siren residents, enjoyed going into the Pour House. It was one of those small town places where everyone knew one another.

Greg Hunter and his wife, Sue, had run the restaurant and bar for the last six years. Just recently, they had re-paved the parking lot, and totally remodeled the inside. Greg cared a lot about the business, and knew a lot about it, too. He and Sue had purchased it from Greg's parents, Bill and Jan Hunter, who, except for a brief year-and-a-half period, had owned it since 1979.

Clark was kind of a storm nut. As he sat there at the Pour House the night of the tornado, he was watching the TV and sky. When he opened the door and looked out to the west, he saw a wall cloud. It looked like a huge giant black wall, coming right at them. He could also see debris flying on the west side of town, and heard what sounded like a huge vacuum. All the people in the bar were complaining that their ears were popping. Then the building blew up. They headed for the beer cooler. Clark saw the roof lift up and blow away. The walls moved out and back in again. Clark and two other people, Chris Cormell and Jeremy Fleischacker, were in the beer cooler; another eight in the food cooler. Clark and the others held on for dear life. The bartender, Chris Cormell, was hanging on to Clark's waist. Clark was worried Chris would blow away. Chris was starting to be pulled up. Clark had his body in a sort of football stance. (He thinks that may have helped him stay on the ground.) Then giant hailstones came, about the size of cantaloupes. From start to finish, he thinks it was 45–60 seconds. Miraculously, no one was injured.

Owner Greg Hunter was four miles away at his house when the tornado hit. Greg had worked the day shift, and gone home before he knew severe weather was approaching. After seeing the tornado warning on TV, he went outside on the deck. From there, he could see the storm approaching. Sitting there that night, Greg kept thinking, "someone in Siren is getting hit." But he did not realize the magnitude of the storm, or that his place of business was directly in the path of the tornado.

He probably wouldn't have even gone into town that night, but he was a volunteer firefighter. His pager had kept going off, urging everyone who possibly could, to come to town to help. Greg's house was east of town, just off County Road B. As he tried to get to Siren, he realized B was covered with trees. He and some other guys spent the better part of an hour clearing a path along B. "I had to cut my way all the way into town," Greg says.

He first saw his business at 9:30 Monday night. Half the building was totally gone, and there was a car parked upside down on the remaining part. The ceiling above the bar area had collapsed on top of it. But full bottles of beer were there; they hadn't spilled. "It was hard for me to believe that everybody had walked away," Greg says, "basically without a scratch." After checking the building himself, to be sure everyone was out, Greg helped Dan and LaWanda McMonagle, who lived behind the Pour House and rented from his parents. The tornado had completely destroyed the house. Greg took them to spend the night at his parents' place, then went back to the Pour House, trying to salvage anything left of value.

The next day, Greg's wife, Sue, went to town and got her first look at the destruction. She was overwhelmed by the number of people there already helping. All sorts of emotions were running through her—shock, sadness, relief that no was hurt.

Her two boys were also with her that morning. Three-year-old Garret walked in with her, and then walked right back out, went to the truck and started looking for something. When she asked him what he was doing, he told her he was, "looking for quarters so he could play

the Big Buck machine." The fact that half of the building was gone and the rest was in ruins didn't phase him. He could see that the video machine was still standing and he wanted to play it.

Six-year-old Asa was sad that his parents' business was gone. But he was also glad that he could still go home to his own house. Sue's family came and picked up the boys for the rest of the week—something for which she was very grateful so that she could help with the clean up.

Volunteers came crawling out of the woodwork that day to help; about 20 people were there, running around in every direction. The Hunters had lots of help but really didn't know where to start. Greg jokes that it was organized chaos.

Two weeks after the tornado, the old building was torn down to make way for the new. Greg misses the people who used to stop in at the bar. He used to see some of them daily. Now he doesn't see them at all. But for the moment, he's looking to the future, concentrating on rebuilding. That helps keep his mind off the loss. The silver lining, he says, is that he gets to fix all of the problems he complained about.

Sue still has mixed emotions about what happened. Rebuilding is a major project. They are in the planning stages for the new building right now (three months after the tornado). She has a big role in designing the kitchen and dining room areas. She is excited because she knows "the new building will be better and have much more to offer the town of Siren."

As for Clark, his 88 Olds was totaled in the storm. Had he driven his 57 Chevy that night, it most certainly would have been destroyed as well.

Dan McMonagle, sitting in what was left of his home east of the Pour House on Third Avenue, the day after the tornado. Photo courtesy of St. Paul Pioneer Press.

Mother Nature's Wrath

"I felt everything being lifted up and I screamed for Dan to hang onto the door along with me. But then we were lifted up about 3 feet. The roaring stopped and we fell to the floor."

—Lawanda McMonagle, Siren Resident

By Lawanda McMonagle

Lawanda and Dan McMonagle had been living in Siren for nine years. The retired couple liked the community a lot. A quiet, friendly town, Lawanda thought. Not too big, but big enough that you could get anything you needed right in town. They rented a house on the north end of the village, right behind the Pour House bar and restaurant. It had six rooms, a one-car garage, and a nice large garden.

The day of the tornado had been a great one. Lawanda, 60, was out of the house all day working in the yard and garden, and putting things away into the garage from a yard sale she had over the weekend.

They were both in the house watching television when the electricity went out at 7:45 P.M. They were looking out the back windows at a large, flat, black, oval-shaped cloud heading at them. But the cloud didn't have a tail. And, as Lawanda pointed out to Dan, "It's moving so fast it just might go past us."

Lawanda went and looked out the front door and there was baseball-size hail coming down; that's when she yelled for Dan, 63, to get into the bathroom. They just raced to the bathroom door and sat on the floor. "When the roaring sound came, the door flew in on us, the ceiling came down, then the wall shifted and the roof came down on us," Lawanda would later recall. "Then, along with the roaring sound, we heard the breaking of wood and glass. I felt everything being lifted up and I screamed for Dan to hang onto the door along with me. But then we were lifted up about 3 feet. The roaring stopped and we fell to the floor."

Dan looked up over the door, which was lying on top of them, and said, "We still have a ceiling!" Lawanda looked up and responded, "Look again . . . it's the sky." It was as white as the ceiling had been.

"Then I heard the crack of metal and heard a 'ssss' noise, along with the smell of gas," Lawanda said. "I knew then that we had to get out of that smashed in bathroom. As of right now, that is the last thing that I remember. You would swear it went on for an hour, but it was only about 30 seconds." After the storm, the sky was blue and white and beautiful. The town, on the other hand, had trees and houses down, and you could not even walk anywhere for fear of electrical wires. The McMonagles went to what used to be their backyard and started yelling for their neighbor who was in a wheelchair. The people from the Pour House came running to pull her out of her house.

Dan and Lawanda went to the Pour House parking lot and it started getting black outside and raining. Some young man gave Lawanda his leather coat because all she had on was her bath robe; a man got out of their car and gave Dan his shoes before continuing on in his own journey to see if his house was still standing. A big black cloud was coming in again and Lawanda panicked. Someone put Dan and Lawanda into their car and drove them to the Pheasant Inn, a bar and restaurant just a few blocks away that had not been destroyed. After the cloud passed, the McMonagles went across the street to the Holiday gas station and the manager let Lawanda in to get cigarettes and a lighter. Then they went to Main Street Market's parking lot, where the emergency command center was set up. Everyone there was just waiting. So they went back to the Pour House parking lot to see the house. The only thing that was left standing at all, was the smashed in bathroom, where they had taken cover during the twister.

The McMonagles' landlords, Siren residents, Bill and Jan Hunter, were out of town. So their son, Greg Hunter, the owner of the Pour House, brought Lawanda and Dan to his parents' house, a block away. "It seemed like it took us an hour to get there with all of the trees blocking the street and other houses blown all over the street," Lawanda said. "Greg checked the house over; it was also in bad shape, although we did not know how bad until daylight."

The McMonagles went back to their property at 5 A.M. The town looked like it had been bombed. They found some of their medications, and some of their clothes. The car had no windows; a 15-foot water pipe jabbed through it. At about 5:30 A.M. the news crews started showing up. Lawanda talked to all of them. "I told them all that I was looking for someone to blame, but there was no one to blame except Mother Nature," Lawanda said. "She's a bitch." Lawanda also told them that you can't even begin to understand what going through a tornado is like, or the fear that you feel, until you experience it yourself.

At 11:00 A.M. that morning, Dan had a hard time breathing, so they went to the Main Street Market parking lot to an ambulance. Dan had lost the nebulizer (a special machine that sprays a liquid mist) he used at home to help him breathe. They put him on a breathing machine. They also put Lawanda's arm in a splint, concerned it might be fractured. (Later, they found out it wasn't.) When they went back to the property they just sat down; they couldn't do any more. A policeman from Osceola, about an hour from Siren, came over and said he had just arrived. He asked if he could help. Lawanda told the policeman she had given up, figuring if anything was left it was all underneath the fallen walls. Lawanda was just too exhausted to care anymore.

Soon that same policeman returned with two more officers and two trucks. They hooked up to the walls and moved them over. Big tears began to roll down Lawanda's cheeks. The officer asked Lawanda if there was anything special she wanted to find. She told him her cat and purse. It took them about five minutes to find her purse, but there was no cat. "I guess it's a woman's thing, my purse and keys," Lawanda said. "Two days later I realized that I didn't have a car or house to use the keys."

Dan and Lawanda just sat there, knowing they had lost everything. Then, all of a sudden, there were about fifteen people on the property picking up things Lawanda didn't know they had. They put things they found on a pickup truck and took it all to their friends' home, Harold and Char Flygstad. About three truckloads in all. They also saw to it that the rest of the news people stayed away. "I just couldn't talk to them anymore without crying and losing my breath," Lawanda recalls. The people from the pet shop came by to try to find her cat, Dusty. They're still looking for him. National Geographic showed up and asked Lawanda if they could film the volunteers. "I said go to it, without these people I would have nothing. I had to throw away about 75% of what they found, but they did all that work and I have a lot of things that meant a lot to my husband and me. The cameraman for National Geographic slipped me $40, and then did not even wait for a thank you."

"The effects of the storm were horrible; we will never, in our lifetime, see all those trees again. The effect on me is that I have never in my lifetime been so afraid of anything or anyone. Now I will always be afraid of dark clouds. What I will miss most is having a home to live in; it's altogether different in an apartment.

"Emotionally I still hear a roar when I close my eyes. And in my mind I can see the spinning, and dark clouds that make me hide. Right now I cope by trying to keep myself busy, and trying to find my cat. Siren will recover because the people are strong willed and will pull together."

Quick Thinking

"It looked like somebody had thrown a bomb in the room."

—*Joel Struck, Siren Resident*

By Nancy Jappe

Siren resident Joel Struck had just gotten home from golfing. He could hear thunder, and hurried to get into the house. There were no warnings on TV at that time. The family ordered a pizza from Kris' Pheasant Inn, a restaurant just down the street.

Joel's wife, Cary, headed to the bathroom to take a shower. Struck told her she'd better not do that. Hail had been falling. Struck found a chunk of it the size of a volleyball. "This is what gave us the warning; we heard the hail," he said. Just before the power went off, he also caught a warning on television. They figured they weren't going to get their pizza after all.

Struck told the family to get into the basement. In their hurry, his boys, Ryan and Aaron, grabbed the dog, but not their baby sister, Heather, who was in her crib. Struck picked up Heather, and handed her to Cary at the foot of the basement steps. He didn't make it down the steps himself before the tornado hit. "It was like standing next to a train," Struck thought. "When the roof went off, it was like a snowstorm. It was hard to breathe because the insulation was so thick in the air."

After the tornado had passed, Struck went outside. It was raining debris. Struck had lived in earthquake-prone California for 13 years. Part of living there was learning how to properly shut off the gas after an earthquake. In California, a wrench is usually tied to the gas meter so people don't have to waste time hunting for one. Although his home and business were destroyed, Struck could smell gas everywhere. Instinct kicked in. While he doesn't remember telling Cary to stay in the basement or grabbing his video camera to film his house, he does remember heading across the yard of his house on Highway 35/70, south of Main Street Market, to the opposite side of the highway.

Struck could hear the whistling of gas, and could follow the smell when he got to First Avenue, on the west side of the highway. Because the power was out, he wasn't as concerned about a fire, but still worried vehicles coming in could give off sparks and cause the gas to explode. People walking around smoking were also a big threat. He yelled at people to put out their cigarettes. For the next 45 minutes, he had to climb over trees or go up over debris, as he turned off the gas at numerous homes and businesses around town. (Struck's efforts likely helped avert a fire or explosion from the leaking gas. A regional manager for the Wisconsin Gas Company, Brian Fay, said it wasn't until 11:15 that night that Wisconsin Gas was able to completely shut off the gas lines to the area.)

Back at home, Struck's son, Ryan, wondered about his car, which had been parked out front. It was totaled. Debris in the yard came from the old Siren Hotel to the west. Most of their furniture never left the house. The kitchen was completely destroyed. "We had a 250 mph stucco job inside and out of our house from the insulation," Struck said. A massive header beam from the hotel went through the window and wall of the master bedroom, just seconds after Cary had left it. "It looked like somebody had thrown a bomb in the room," Struck said. "There were broken pictures on the walls."

Their business, Joel's Bait Shop, was attached to their home. All that was left of the four-door beer cooler were the two doors. The rest of the cooler and everything in it were gone.

They never found a canoe that was in the back yard. Struck's boat was found wrapped around a tree to the east several blocks away. Later, he put it on Main Street, attaching a sign "for sale, cheap" on the tangled mass. Struck figured half the family's belongings went north, and the other half east.

The Strucks couldn't believe what the town looked like. It was as if they were in a war-torn country. "It was overwhelming," Struck said. He found himself getting lost because familiar landmarks weren't there any more.

The family ended up saving a lot of junk because they didn't know what else to do with it. Colonial Craft donated a semi for them to use to store their personal possessions. They put everything in, with the thought of sorting later. The family had just purchased a lot in a new subdivision in the village and planned to build a house there.

They worried about looting after the curfew was lifted. Too many people around. People with video cameras taking pictures, upset Struck, as did members of the media who walked right into his house without permission.

But there were many positives after the storm as well. Like all the people who poured into town to volunteer their time. Struck had so many people offering to help, that he actually had to turn some away. More than half came from the Twin Cities.

Twelve years ago, Struck and his family sold everything, left California and headed back to Wisconsin. Dealing with the aftermath of the tornado is, for the Struck family, like when they first moved back: It's a time for starting all over. "Things don't get done overnight," Struck said. "You have to have a lot of patience."

One of the first things that needed to be done the night of the tornado was to turn off the gas. "There could have been some bad situations from the time of the storm to turning (the gas) off. Who knew? So many lines were down. I treated every one as if it was hot," Struck commented.

As it got light the morning after the tornado, Struck could see all the helicopters and planes flying overhead—overwhelming numbers, stacking up two or three high. He was amazed there wasn't an air accident. "No matter where you looked, there were vehicles in the sky," he said. "My own world was the block just where my house was. I knew other areas were destroyed, but there was no way to get to see it."

At 5 A.M., Struck got away long enough to go east, behind the Pour House, a popular restaurant and bar in Siren. He saw Lawanda and Dan McMonagle at a table on the slab where their house had stood. The only thing left on the slab was the table, and a little bit of wall that used to be part of the kitchen. "The McMonagles were crying," Struck said. Something he hadn't been able to do yet.

Under the Rubble

"I felt us falling in slow motion and could see nothing but gray. I knew the front walls were pushing and falling in on us."

—*Cindy Blaker, Siren Resident*

By Jill Gloodt and Chad Thomas

It was a lazy summer evening, and Cindy Blaker was at her Siren home with her husband, Dick. The Blakers were enjoying a quiet night parked on the couch, married just two months before. While Dick watched television, Cindy rested her eyes. One of the last things she heard before nodding off was the TV weather folks on the air. They were talking about storms sweeping across Minnesota and into northwestern Wisconsin. But that's the way it had been for weeks. It storms this time of year, Cindy thought, nothing unusual.

But while Cindy slept, Dick could see the weather outside worsening, causing the power to go off. Dick eventually became alarmed enough to decide they needed to move to a safer spot in the house. A drowsy Cindy would awaken to Dick's yelling, telling her the weather was bad and to get into the hallway.

As Cindy rose from the couch and got into her wheelchair, she looked outside and saw a black strip of clouds with a hook hanging down. Her ears popped, and she knew they were in trouble.

Rushing into the hallway, Cindy slammed open her daughter Naomi's bedroom door, and instructed the 17 year old to join them. Her husband just made it. All the time Cindy's ears were popping and plugging. And then, Cindy recalls, "I felt us falling in slow motion and could see nothing but gray. I knew the front walls were pushing and falling in on us. I was not afraid and did not hear any train. It lasted 3 to 5 seconds in my estimation." (Cindy later learned that while she thought she had been falling in slow motion, she might actually have been flying through the air.) As the rubble continued to land on top of them, they all told each other how much they loved one another. And then as quickly as the tornado had come, it was gone. Cindy knew she was trapped under the rubble. As she glanced over at her husband, Dick, she could also see he was pinned down. A door covered his chest. She was unsure if he was injured. But Naomi was only partially buried; she managed to get free and run to a neighbor's house to call 911.

While Cindy and Dick waited for help to arrive, they clasped hands across the debris and prayed together. Cindy was concerned about her husband. Dick kept saying it was hard for him to breathe. And Cindy thought she could see him bleeding. Making matters worse, Cindy could smell gas. She knew that in the tornado, many of the town's gas lines must have ruptured. Still, she never thought either of them would die. A woman with a deep faith, Cindy says, "I just felt protected."

Not more than 10 minutes later, Cindy figures, rescuers arrived and pulled them out. The wheelchair Cindy was in when the tornado struck was destroyed, and she had no idea how she would get out of there. But then, as she turned around, there was her old wheelchair. Amazingly, while it was a little rickety, it was standing there undamaged. It wasn't even dusty. "Divine intervention," she laughs.

And as Cindy sat there stunned, she says an angel swept in to help. It was the pastor from her church, Steve Ward, who emerged out of the chaos and brought her and Dick to the United Methodist Church in another part of town. There, Pastor Ward and his wife, Gail, gave them dry clothes and bedding. Cindy's daughter, Naomi, went to a friend's house. Throughout the night, Cindy and Dick talked and prayed with the Wards. They also shed a lot of tears.

To Cindy's delight, the next day, as she looked out the window of the Wards' home, her two grown daughters, Natalie and Neela, pulled up. They had rushed to Siren from the Twin Cities with their spouses. Cindy gave them all a big hug. Neela and Naomi left soon thereafter to begin the backbreaking task of sifting through the rubble to find anything that was salvageable. Natalie stayed to comfort Cindy.

Many volunteers also came and pitched in, among them church youth groups. The first on the scene was an old friend of Cindy's, Larry French. He stayed there day after day. "It's amazing the work he put in," Cindy said. "He's just a real good Samaritan."

As they dug through the debris, the Blakers managed to salvage some important pieces of their lives, such as family photographs. But most everything else was gone, including all the beautiful trees. "The scope of the devastation hit me when they were cutting down my trees—a big crane grabbed my wrap-around couch in chunks and I cried. I said goodbye to each loved piece of home he threw away," Cindy said. "It took a lifetime to accumulate books and things and furniture to make my home beautiful—insurance won't pay enough to replace them."

This is all that was left of the Cindy and Dick Blaker home on Third Avenue, Siren, after the tornado passed through. The Blakers were in the house during the tornado, along with Cindy's daughter, Naomi Nelson. Unbelievably, they were not hurt. Photo courtesy of Inter-County Leader.

Photo courtesy of Star Tribune.

Strength for Tomorrow

"With a storm like that, what else is there to do but be strong? Nothing can change an event like a tornado."

—Elna Wambolt, Siren Resident

By Barb Lyga

Elna Wambolt had a serene life in her home on the north end of Siren. The 62-year-old had called Siren home for 37 years, and had numerous friends and family in the area. Her son, Wade, daughter-in-law, Kim, and two granddaughters lived just one block away. She loved spending time with her granddaughters, visiting them nearly every day. They often played cards together, or went shopping.

The night of the tornado, Elna and her husband, Skip, were listening to their scanner at home, and first heard the tornado warnings there. As the storm approached, they sought refuge in their basement. Elna was sure her house would blow away. She could feel it "twisting." And then suddenly it was over. The thought never crossed Elna's mind that she and Skip could have died. It all happened so fast.

When Elna and Skip emerged from the basement, they couldn't believe their eyes. Their house was completely gone. Trees were down all around them. Looking over at their son Wade's house, they could see the new addition was no longer there. But they knew Kim and the girls were at her parents' house.

Despite all the destruction, it was hard for that reality to set in at first. "We can stay here," Skip said. "Our bedroom is okay." They could not imagine where they would go.

Their son, Wade, a volunteer firefighter, was the first person to reach them. When he arrived, Elna was sitting on her porch holding her little dog. Skip was inside. He gave them a big hug and told them they had to leave the area because of leaking gas. They spent the night looking for a place to stay. They eventually found a room at a motel in Luck, about 15 miles south of Siren.

The next day Elna and Skip were tired and confused as they tried to sort out their most important things. People were everywhere, chainsaws going, volunteers helping, and people coming right in to help Elna and Skip pack.

In the weeks after the tornado, Elna felt the constant stress of having no place to call home; she missed her old house and her daily routine. She was saddened when she thought about all the other homes that were lost, and trees that had been toppled, but she has done her best to move on. "With a storm like that, what else is there to do but be strong?" she asks. "Nothing can change an event like a tornado."

Elna has come a long way in the healing process by moving into her new home—plopped down right where her old one was within weeks of the tornado. "It feels good to have a place to call home. As soon as water and electricity were hooked up, we moved in. It was so exciting to see the house set down on its foundation."

Wade, Kim and the girls are back, too. Elna can once again play cards and go shopping with her granddaughters. Now she wants neighbors back. Until then, she can holler out the door to Wade, Kim and the girls because there are no other homes between them. For now, but not for long.

Trapped in the Closet

"Get me out of here!"

—*Siren Resident Jean Marion, after the tornado*

By Jill Gloodt

Dawn Davey woke up the morning of the storm with a feeling of dread. She couldn't explain it. Couldn't get rid of it. That afternoon she ended up calling her sister, Laurie Burington, to talk with her about it. Dawn remembers telling Laurie, "Goodbye, I love you."

That night Dawn and her husband, Dave Davey, were watching television at Dawn's mother's house, on the north end of Siren. They noticed the warnings. There was a tornado in Braham, Minnesota, on its way to Grantsburg, Wisconsin. Directly in the path of the storm after that: Siren, where it would most likely hit around 8:30 P.M.

Dawn told the family they had better get somewhere safe, but her mother's home didn't have a basement. Dawn's mother, Jean Marion, didn't want her daughter to worry. Jean tried to remain calm and told her, "Oh, I've been through these storms before." At first they decided to sit in the bathroom, thinking that would be the safest, but realized the bathroom window might shatter. So they decided to get into the bedroom closet.

They started taking everything out and Jean went in first. If anyone was to be hit, Dawn and Dave didn't want it to be Jean. The closet had no door of its own, but was located close to the bedroom door. So Dave opened the bedroom door and used it best he could to cover the closet opening. The closet was 2 by 3 feet. They were very cramped, but felt fairly safe under the bed quilt they had draped over their heads.

The next thing they remember is their ears either plugging or popping. They began to hear the windows breaking; the walls moving in and out as if they were taking a breath. They could feel the entire house sliding off of its foundation. And they could hear the trees creaking, bending and breaking off. They dared not move. Jean was praying.

Dave took a moment to look out from underneath the blanket. He saw a car caught up in the wind coming straight at their house. Just before it was about to hit, the wind took it and flipped it into the neighbor's yard.

Then came the silence. Dead silence. They all thought for a moment it was over. Jean wanted very much to get out of the closet. Dave said, "No, we better stay here, sometimes the storm comes back." And it did. The wind was whooshing. They heard the roof being taken off, the walls going in and out. Then it was over. This time for good.

They emerged from their tiny closet, checking to make sure they were all alive and unharmed. They didn't have shoes on, so they went to find some. Glass, metal, wood slivers everywhere. The roof was gone, the windows were gone, and the walls were cracked.

Jean had some precious mementos of her husband's (he died in 1959) in a small box inside a glass china cupboard. This cabinet had belonged at one time to her grandmother. It held not only the memorabilia of her husband, but also a set of very old china from her grandmother. As Jean looked around at all the devastation, she was sure her precious things would most likely be gone. But when she checked her china cupboard, she found every dish came through without a scratch. Her only mementos of her husband, dry and unharmed.

They now could smell gas. They knew they had to get out. It took what seemed like forever to escape from the broken home. When they finally did, trees, power lines, glass and cars were everywhere. Their neighbors hollered to them, "Are you ok?" Jean, Dawn and Dave couldn't believe people were alive. They couldn't believe they were alive.

Dawn yelled back, "Thank God, we're all right!" As soon as Dawn's voice began to drop, her mother, Jean, said in a loud voice, "Get me out of here!"

They knew they had to go somewhere safer—somewhere where the gas wasn't leaking. So they began to walk. As they moved along, Dawn said, "Someone must have been really watching over us." Dawn's husband, Dave, smiled and said, "Dawn, I usually don't listen to you as much as I should. (But) after all we've been through, and your premonition, I will now."

They first walked to the Pheasant Inn and asked if they could use their phone. It wasn't working. They made their way amidst all the debris and dazed people to Tom's Bar. There the owner, Gloria Johnson, let them make a call.

They immediately contacted their friends and family to make sure everyone was okay. They were able to reach everyone except Dawn's sister, Laurie Burington. (She was already on her way up to Siren.)

They knew they probably shouldn't because of the downed power lines, but they began to wander around town. This was their hometown, after all. They felt compelled to see what was left of it. They could not believe the devastation. As they continued to wander and wonder where they would spend the night, an emergency worker told them to walk up to the school. They could find shelter there. They arrived at the school and found the open arms of the volunteers and emergency workers.

They sat up all night at the school. Sleep would not come. Dawn's back was hurting. After visiting the emergency room, she was told her back must have been hit by flying debris. She was so thankful that she would heal.

The next morning they realized Dawn's sister, Laurie Burington, had been unable to get into Siren the night of the storm due to all the debris. Laurie did not know if her family was alive or dead. When they did find each other later on the day after the storm, they shared many tears of joy.

Back at the house that day, they worked to

salvage what they could. They found Jean's push lawnmower wedged into one of the walls. As her children were cleaning up, they pulled out the lawnmower and all the nails in the wall popped. The wall started to cave. Dawn and Jean both thought: The lawnmower had held up the wall.

For a few months after the storm, Jean stayed with her daughter. Finally, in September Jean's new doublewide home was delivered. Jean finally had her own place again! It's a bit bigger, but resembles the old house to a large degree with one small exception: Her children insisted this one have a basement!

Ben Anderson, a Frederic sixth-grader at the time, and his father, Dean, a board member of the Burnett Youth Hockey Association, walk through the destruction of the Lodge Center Arena after Ben saw the tornado damage for the first time. "I broke two records in there," Ben, a member of the Burnett Blizzard hockey team, said, with tears in his eyes. "This is for the kids so it has got to be rebuilt," Dean said. "We did it once; we can do it again." Photo courtesy of Inter-County Leader.

Community Pride

"Siren is still a great place to live. Thank God we're alive."

—*Message on T-shirts sold in Siren after the tornado*

By Jill Gloodt

Siren residents Tom and Dawn Anderson had always considered their community a great, wholesome place to raise kids. The town had a real secure and family atmosphere.

The two had long been involved with programs geared toward children, like the Burnett County Youth Hockey Association. Just six weeks before the tornado, in fact, Tom Anderson had become president of the hockey association. While the 50-year-old had been involved with the organization well before taking on that responsibility, he knew this new job would be much more time consuming. But he really didn't mind. He did it for the kids.

Many in Siren were very proud of the town's new indoor ice rink, on the north side of town. It opened in January of 1999. But there were still many odds and ends to clean up, or things to fix at the hockey arena. Tom was often there doing such jobs. The day of the tornado, he was there welding one of the stairways. In the late afternoon, Dawn left with her son, Claire, for a hockey game in Spooner, about 26 miles east of Siren.

Tom stayed at the arena for a meeting at 7 P.M. Three people from Spooner and three from Siren were supposed to attend. But the Spooner people never made it. So after talking until about 7:40, two of the Siren people went home. Tom stayed and worked a little while longer. He eventually got hungry, hot and tired, and decided to head for home as well. It was about 8:15. Ten minutes later the tornado hit Siren, just as Dawn and Claire arrived home from Spooner.

The twister rolled over the top of the ice arena. The building was completely blown apart. After the storm, Tom and his dad, Jerry Anderson, tried a number of ways to get into town. Once they finally did, they saw the devastation, including the hockey rink. Tom said, "Oh my God, dad, take me back home so I can get my chainsaw!" Had Tom and the others been there, they surely would have been killed.

Almost immediately after the storm, hockey association members began working on the hard task of rebuilding. The arena was underinsured. They had enough to get the shell back up, but they needed more for the inside. So they did as they had before, they started fundraising.

They sold special hockey pucks as tornado souvenirs. Then Peggy Strabel, Siren Chamber of Commerce President, had a wonderful plan. Her idea was to make T-shirts that read on the front, "Siren is still a great place to live." On the back, "Thank God we're alive." The T-shirts raised more than $5,500 in just three short weeks. They also served a therapeutic purpose for the proud people of Siren, still reeling from what had happened. As the T-shirts began showing up all over town, the message was loud and clear: Together, as they had in the past, residents would get through this tragedy too.

Reconstruction of the rink is already well underway.

"What I'm taking away from the storm," Dawn says, "is the knowledge that there are some giving and wonderful people in this world!"

Tornado Fears Linger On

"I still have terror at times. It comes and gets you in the face."

—*Joan Phillips, Siren Resident*

By Nancy Jappe

From her temporary apartment in Shell Lake, Wisconsin, Joan Phillips recounts with vivid detail the events of the night of the tornado. At the time, the 67 year old was living in the back building of Birchwood Manor, Siren's senior citizen apartment complex. Her apartment was the only one in the 25-unit complex that was not destroyed. However, unlike the other residents in the building, she spent the two days after the tornado at Spooner Hospital.

Phillips was not injured in the tornado. She went through the terrifying experience lying on a blanket, her face and upper body covered by a pillow, in her storeroom a couple doors south of her apartment. However, while sitting at Kris' Pheasant Inn, a restaurant and bar in the center of Siren, after being rescued from the totally destroyed building, Phillips felt shock symptoms. Her oxygen supply was running low, and she asked to be taken to the hospital. At the Spooner Hospital (Spooner is 26 miles east of Siren) she was treated for respiratory problems and anxiety. The morning after she was admitted, the nurses found her bed was full of pink insulation. It was in her

hair and all over her body. Two days after the tornado, she was got out of the hospital, and went to stay with her granddaughter, Amber Remakul, who lives in the Twin Cities.

"I still have terror at times. It comes and gets you in the face," Phillips says, two months after the tornado. "The first thing I said (after leaving the storeroom) was, it looks like we were hit by a bomb." She refused to look around town, or to view other areas of destruction.

In an ironic twist to her story, about two weeks before the tornado, Phillips had Jan Lenz, her housekeeper for the past 10 years, put the quilt, pillow and small extra tank of oxygen in the storeroom. Lenz was going on vacation. Phillips wanted protection, just in case bad weather, or a tornado, should strike.

On the morning of June 18, Phillips was in a good mood. It was a beautiful day, and she was singing a hymn and feeling wonderful. Later on, in the early evening, she was talking to her friend in Siren, Barb Murphy, on the telephone. She could hear the Murphys' scanner in the background, with the dispatcher giving a warning that a tornado had gone through

Alpha, and was about seven minutes from Siren.

Phillips headed toward the storeroom, returning once to her apartment to get a glass of water. She laid down on the quilt, and put the pillow over her head. At first, she heard the sound of hail. "I can live with that. It's not going to hurt anything," Phillips said to herself. She also wondered about the chance of a tornado hitting her building, back in the woods as it was.

Then the tornado struck. "I felt like I was being compressed in a vacuum, squished, terrible pressure," she said. The feeling was over in about three minutes, minutes that felt like an eternity. She could hear people in the hallway and knew the experience was over.

The residents of the other apartments, along with a neighbor girl, gathered in the building's party room. From there, law enforcement personnel took them to the Pheasant Inn. "I was only wearing a short nightgown," Phillips said. "People said, 'If you ran back for water, why didn't you get your robe?' I thought I would be going right back to my apartment, and that no one would see me. Here I was, sitting in the Pheasant Inn in a nighty. A lady there gave me a blouse (that was too small) and some socks."

Three or four people from Phillips' building were at the Pheasant Inn. None were hurt, but they were covered by insulation. They sat there for quite awhile. A man asked Phillips if she wanted anything. By that time, she was feeling the signs of shock and need for hospital attention.

Phillips had lived at Birchwood Manor for more than four years. Her parents had a cabin on Crooked Lake during her childhood years, and were frequent visitors to the area. Siren has always been near and dear to Phillips, and is now the town she calls home. Once Birchwood Manor is rebuilt, Phillips will be right back in her apartment. Almost all of her belongings were salvaged, except for her white rugs (soaked by 3-4 inches of water when the water pipes in the hallway ruptured), curtains and shades. In the meantime, Phillips is making do in her temporary housing and dealing with the effects of her tornado experience.

Feeling the need to talk about what happened, she is seeing a psychologist. "I was so scared," she said. When it rains, or when she hears the Shell Lake fire siren go off, she is transported back to that storeroom on June 18. At first, when the fire siren would go off, she would call 911, asking anxiously, "Is a tornado coming?"

That feeling of anxiety still persists three months after the tornado. "I never thought anything like that would ever happen to me," Phillips said. "If anybody thinks they are just going to get over it, they are wrong. I don't think I will ever feel super safe again."

Above the fear, she is grateful that no one was killed in the building, and no one was seriously injured. She is also grateful for forethought, and for Lenz putting the quilt, pillow and oxygen in the storeroom. Just in case. "I wasn't taking any chance," Phillips said. "I put a plan into action and it worked!"

A Good Samaritan

"I am thankful I wasn't hurt and was able to help other people after the storm."

—*Venita Hill, Siren Resident*

By Jill Gloodt

There are many people who spend their entire lives in Siren. And many more who move away, but are pulled back to the place where they grew up. Drawn to return by the small town's friendly atmosphere.

Sixty-three-year-old Venita Hill was one of those people who left and came back. She graduated from Webster High School in 1955, and returned many years later after she retired. Venita had many friends still in Siren and wanted once again to live in the area. That's part of what made living in Siren again so enjoyable. Venita had many friends to visit. She also had a comfortable apartment in a complex for seniors on the north end of town. The place filled with many pictures and personal things she had collected throughout the years.

As Venita recalls it, it was very hot and muggy the day of the tornado. But that didn't prevent her from doing her regular things, such as taking a walk to pick up the mail. She went out to Hertel that evening, about 15 miles east of Siren, for dinner with her sister, Velores Taylor, and her family.

Around 7:30 P.M. she headed back into town.

She turned on the TV and saw the storm warnings. Her sister had seen them, too. Venita's sister called, suggesting that Venita return to Hertel so she would be safe with family. But Venita thought it best to stay at her apartment. She didn't want to be on the road when the storm hit.

As the tornado moved into Siren, Venita was in her apartment, the warnings continuing to flash on television for people to take cover. Instead of doing that, however, Venita went outside to check for herself. It was real still at first. But by the time she got back into her apartment, the trees were starting to roll. Venita grabbed a flashlight, went into the bathroom and held the door shut. It seemed like it lasted a long time, she thought, but it was less than 5 minutes. The experience was petrifying.

"I was really scared. The sound was really loud," Venita recalled later. "The roof was coming off. The bathroom ceiling fell in and then it rained and hailed. I waited a few minutes and then opened the door."

Venita had to crawl over debris to get out of her apartment. She could hear voices in the hallway, and instinctively went to help. There were two people when she first got there. One was on oxygen and dressed in a nightgown. Venita told the woman to wait there, while she went to get some other clothes for her. Venita didn't want the woman to cut herself in case there were glass shards on the floor. When Venita got back to her own apartment, she could see water everywhere. The pipes had burst. She ignored that for now, and gathered up some clothes and shoes for the woman in the hallway. She then brought that woman to the building's community room.

After that, Alice Mavis, an elderly Siren woman, who used a walker, needed help, so Venita brought her back to her apartment so that she could get her medicine. By the time help arrived, Venita had brought three others to the community room as well. The six of them huddled there together.

Emergency crews later took the others to the emergency operations center in the middle of town, but Venita walked from her apartment to Siren's Methodist Church and called another one of her sisters, who lives out on Old 35, on the western edge of town. Venita walked about a mile out of town, and her sister picked her up from there. Venita's daughter, Renee Roberts, who had been frantically trying to check on her mom and aunts, finally reached everyone. She drove up from Milltown south of Siren, and brought them all back there.

The next day Renee took Venita back to her apartment, and she salvaged what she could; everything was wet and covered with insulation. Her apartment had caved in. But through it all she's tried to keep her sense of humor as well. When she met Wisconsin Governor Scott McCallum, who had come to Siren to assess the damage, she joked to her kids that they should have given her time to fix her hair first for the special occasion.

Two months after the storm, Venita was still living with her daughter in Milltown, 23 miles south of Siren. While the storm took many of her material possessions and her nice apartment, what she misses most is the regular contact with her friends and family in Siren. She can't wait to get back to town once the apartment building is rebuilt. But she knows that will take some time

"I try to keep busy and not think about what I have lost. I am more fortunate than people who lost everything," Venita says. "I am thankful I wasn't hurt and was able to help other people after the storm."

Venita had always wondered how she'd react in an emergency situation. But like many of the heroes that night, she just did what had to be done without thinking about it. "I guess I am surprised I was capable of this. I know God must have given me a little boost and let me know I needed to do this."

A Mother's Prayer

"I prayed to God that Marci would be alive!"

—Siren Resident Cindy Johnson, on the search for her daughter

By Cindy Johnson

It was the evening of Monday, June 18 about 7:30 P.M. I had just gotten home from cleaning the Siren Dental Office when the phone rang. It was my mom, Ethel Peterson. She wanted to make sure I knew there was a tornado watch for our area. We usually watch satellite TV, so are oblivious to bad weather information on local television. In turn, I called both of my daughters, Amy and Marci, to relay Grandma's message. I then switched the TV to a local station to watch the weather warnings. I called the girls a couple of times just to check in with them.

About 8:10 P.M., my husband, Rodney, decided to take his evening shower. I was busy watching the weather when I noticed the grass in the field swirling in all directions. I got off the couch for a better look. Trees by our pond were swaying. I heard an oo-oo-oo sound. "Train? Tornado!" I thought. I yelled for Rodney to get out of the shower. Just then our power went out.

Rodney came waltzing out of the bathroom in a towel. I screamed, "I think it's a tornado!" We headed for the basement steps, but by then everything had calmed down and we never even went down there. We took a look outside. One branch from our poplar tree was lying in the driveway. This was a typical loss in our yard whenever we've had a storm. "No big deal, " we thought. Rod turned on the radio, but he couldn't get any station to come in. Without power, our portable phone didn't work, so I couldn't call anyone.

We decided to go to bed. I couldn't sleep. I tossed and turned for about 10 minutes when Rod suggested I drive to town to check on the girls. I thought that if I knew everything was OK, I'd be able to sleep. As I got dressed, I realized I didn't know how to make the garage door opener work when there's no power. So back to bed I went.

After another five minutes of tossing and turning, I asked Rodney to drive me to town in his truck. I could hear sirens going. I'm sure my woman's intuition was pushing me. He was reluctant, but put on his bathrobe, with no shoes. I got dressed for a second time and we headed for town.

About one mile from our house, trees were covering County Road B (a road that heads into

Siren from the east). We had to drive in the ditch. Our first stop was at Amy's house. My heart was pounding. We had to drive under a broken off tree that was arched over the driveway. Amy wasn't home, but Rodney noticed fresh car tracks. We decided she and Chad Alden, her roommate, must have gone to Siren.

We continued towards town. Fallen pine trees by Long Lake Road (about a mile out of town) were blocking most of B. So we headed for the ditch again. Lillian Morse's property was devastated. There was a vehicle in the ditch with its lights flashing. I think this is when I knew Siren had had a tornado. As we got closer to town, which seemed like a lifetime to get there, I noticed hundreds of flashing lights ahead. I prayed to God that Marci would be alive and also thanked Him that I wasn't driving!

We turned on 4th Street by the school (on the eastern side of town). There was no way we were going to get to Marci's house. Rodney angled on different side streets. It was hopeless to get to Marci's. We then decided to go to my Mom's house and check on her. She lives on Highway 70 just West of the Jehovah Witness Hall.

As we pulled in her driveway, trees were down everywhere, blocking our entry. As I ran to her house, it was then that I noticed her garage had also gone down with her car inside. She came out of the house. We hugged and cried. I was so thankful she was OK. Then the next best thing happened. She told me Marci had just been there to check on her. I then knew Marci was okay, too!

By then Rodney had gotten out of the truck to look the situation over. I'm sure he was wishing he had gotten dressed or at least put on shoes. After walking around my mom's yard, we headed home.

As we parked the truck, there was Marci, her boyfriend, Dan, and her two cats. "Thank you, God!" I said. With candles and a lantern lit, we listened to Marci's story. After that we went to bed, but I never did sleep that night.

Disbelief

"Oh, my God, I can't believe this is happening!"

—*Marci Johnson, Siren Resident*

By Nancy Daniels

Marci Johnson lived on D'Jock Street in a rental house on the north end of town, not far from the Pour House restaurant and bar. The night of the tornado she had been watching the news with her boyfriend, Dan Goranson. They heard a tornado was headed toward Siren, but really didn't think it would get that far. Marci was making muffins. After they were done baking, she and Dan planned to go for a car ride.

But the weather started to look a little worse, so Marci lit a candle. Then the power went out. Dan was looking out the door and saw the tornado coming. It was so very loud and sounded like a train. Their ears popped and things started

Siren resident Marci Johnson is consoled by her boyfriend, Dan Goranson. Photo courtesy of St. Paul Pioneer Press.

flying. Dan quickly shut off the gas oven, before both of them dashed into a small crawlspace in the bedroom. The house lifted and shifted. The stairs to the crawlspace moved. All Marci could think was, "Oh, my God, I can't believe this is happening!"

It was over in just minutes. They both wondered: "Should we go up?" One of their two cats was in the crawlspace with them, but the other one was not. Dan wanted to go to find it. But Marci was apprehensive. After all was quiet, they did finally head upstairs, but both of them had to crawl out of the front door to get out of the house. They found their other cat upstairs. It was also unharmed.

Once they were outside they smelled gas and could hear it leaking. They wanted to make sure the neighbors were okay. Everyone they checked on was. They walked around in a daze. They just couldn't believe what had happened. They saw Siren Police Chief Dean Roland and firemen checking on people. Marci was very worried about her grandma, Ethel Peterson, who lived on the west side of Siren on Highway 70, so she walked about a mile through the town to check on her. When she approached her grandma's home, she was relieved to see her standing outside. They hugged and then looked around at the damage. Her grandma had lost a lot of trees, and her garage had collapsed. Before the tornado hit, her grandma had gone down into the basement just to shut a window. When she came up the tornado had passed, without her even knowing it.

After hugging again, and telling her grandma that she loved her, Marci headed back to town to find Dan. It was getting dark. She was also worried about her cats. She walked up and down the streets, not really knowing or believing where she was. It was starting to rain. About an hour and half after leaving her house, Marci finally found Dan and the cats. They knew they couldn't spend the night in the house. All of the windows had blown in, and the rain was pouring down.

They were eventually able to make it out to Marci's parents' house. They spent what little there was left of the night there. The next morning they were up early to check on the house and their cars. Everything was totaled. Marci had left her wallet in her car and it had been stolen. Nothing in the house had been taken. They worked for three days to salvage what they could from the house and garage. The garage blew away and they still haven't found it. Many things were stored out there in boxes. All of it, completely gone.

The Salvation Army and Fingerhut donated many things to help replace some of what was lost: Something for which Marci is very grateful. She misses her neighbors and doesn't know where she'll relocate. For now she is still living with her parents. She knows she never wants to see that kind of destruction again.

Oh, and the muffins turned out just perfect. The next morning they ate one.

❧

Disorientation

"Everything I had used as a marker was gone. I even walked right past my own driveway."

—*Connie Keith, Siren Resident*

By Connie Keith

I was getting ready for work when my kids saw on the TV that there was severe weather. It looked like it was going to go over Grantsburg, where I work at Parker Hannifan, a manufacturing plant. (Grantsburg is 15 miles west of Siren.) The kids were worried about where I would go if the weather turned ugly. I assured them I would be safe at work.

My daughter, Stephanie, told Peggy, the person with whom I ride to work, that bad weather was coming. As Peg and I were driving, we didn't come upon clouds until just east of Falun (an unincorporated town between Siren and Grantsburg). Peggy watched the road, as I watched the sky for the storm. It looked as if the storm was more towards the north, and that maybe Webster was going to get the most of it. (Webster is six miles north of Siren.) The sky was very dark leaving Falun. The wind was starting to pick up.

The whole sky was turning as we came up to Alpha (nine miles west of Siren). Just after we drove through Alpha, I looked to the north and saw two large animals, one right behind the other, in the air above a barn heading straight for Siren. Two days later, I found out that these animals were cows from a nearby farm. (They belonged to Joe and Virginia Hennessey.) Sheets of metal were coming off the barn and following the animals. At this point it looked like a black wall of clouds. Seeing the animals stunned me. I didn't even think that this was a tornado.

The wind was very strong, but Peggy kept the car on the road. I noticed a small car coming towards us, and I thought it had a bike on the roof. I told Peg, "I hope that bike doesn't come off and hit our windshield." When the small car got closer, I realized it had antennas and a satellite dish on the roof. There were two more cars right behind the first one, equipped the same way. I told Peggy they were storm chasers. Rain was coming down in heavy sheets and it was hard to see. Some vehicles had pulled off to the side of the road.

Then, by the time we got to the Grantsburg High School, the rain had stopped and the sun was shining. We stopped at Amoco in Grantsburg and heard on the scanner that a tornado just hit Falun. When we got to work, Peg and I called home to let our families know about the storm coming and that we were fine.

I was calm calling home because I still thought the storm would be north of Siren. I was not prepared to hear my husband, Chuck, with a frantic devastated voice tell me that he and the kids were okay, but that we had lost everything. The house had trees on it, that also went through my boys' bedroom ceiling and north wall. The boys, Ryan and Eric, had a bunk bed. If this storm had hit at night while they were sleeping, we would surely have lost Ryan.

A co-worker, Margo, offered to take me back to Siren. She lived in Falun and wanted to check on her children. Getting back into Siren was not easy. Highway 70 (the main road into Siren from Grantsburg) had been closed off. So we headed down some back roads to the south of Siren. These roads were also closed. I had Margo drop me off. I started walking to my aunt's house on the south side of Siren. It was still raining, there were downed power lines and trees, and there was no power.

I made it to my Aunt Myrtle Snow's house about 10:00 that night. This was as far as I could go. A police officer brought my three children to me about 11:30. I finally heard again from my husband by phone around midnight. He stayed at our house to protect it. After hugging and holding my kids for a long time, I was able to calm down and sleep until 4:30 in the morning. I then got up and walked home. As I walked down 4th Avenue, I was shocked by what I saw. I even had to stop and figure out where I was because I felt lost. Everything I had used as a marker was gone. I even walked right past my own driveway. It looked like a jungle. I had to climb over many huge oak trees to get to my house. I found Chuck, and all I could do was cry.

We lost 26 out of 28 trees, mostly huge oaks. Our vehicles, shed and house were destroyed. By 7:00 that next morning, there were already many friends, neighbors and relatives helping us clean up.

We are now in the process of rebuilding our home. We are very thankful to God that he protected our family and many others in the Siren community. We are also thankful for all the volunteers, the Red Cross and Salvation Army. And we are especially thankful for our family and friends.

A Hard Lesson

"My house is gone. I grew up in that house. I learned I really don't like storms at all."

—*Ryan Keith, 13-year-old Siren Resident*

By Jill Gloodt

Thirteen-year-old Ryan Keith thought the weather looked gloomy the night of the tornado. He had been out that evening driving with his dad, Chuck Keith. By the time they got back to their home on South Shore Drive in Siren (on the north end of the village), the clouds looked like a big black wall, turning and turning. He ran to the Crooked Lake beach with his 7-year-old sister, Stephanie. They saw green clouds spinning. Frightened, they ran home and went into the basement.

There, Ryan heard a train sound and lots of trees hitting his house. Ryan said he was so scared. After the trees began falling on the house, Ryan blocked everything else out, not remembering what happened until after the tornado had passed.

Chuck Keith and his three children (Ryan also has a 9-year-old brother Eric) knew they had to get help. They began walking as best they could amidst the debris until they reached the Lodge, a hotel on the north end of Siren, near Crooked Lake. They sat there, waiting for permission to continue their journey to see if their grandmother, Myrtle Snow, was okay. (Myrtle Snow is actually the children's great aunt. But they have always called her grandma.) The children were so tired, and the wait so long, that they fell asleep on the back of a fire truck. Chuck was growing impatient. He was told to head to Main Street Market in the center of town; maybe he could catch a ride there to check on Grandma Snow. He woke up the children and they walked to the market, where the emergency personnel had set up their command post. There, Chuck asked an emergency worker for a ride. Within an hour, they were finally at Grandma Snow's house. She was fine. "We're alright. We're going to make it," Ryan told his grandmother. "I love you."

The next day was like a dream to Ryan. (The tornado had completely destroyed the Keiths' home.) Ryan remembers helping his dad cut trees at his home and at grandma's, trying to get the brush out of the way. He felt that maybe he was a little in shock. He couldn't believe a tornado had really come to Siren. His yard once had 28 trees, now only two were left. For many days after that Ryan and his family tried to pick up what was left of their home and yard.

"I will never forget the storm," Ryan says. "I will miss the shade and the trees. I sometimes am depressed about this. My house is gone. I grew up in that house. I learned I really don't like storms at all."

Signs of Faith

"We are here. God is here. We are blessed."

—Sign in front of Bethany Lutheran Church after tornado

By Pastor Diane Blahauvietz, Larry Blahauvietz and Chad Thomas

Since moving to Siren to serve as pastor at Bethany Lutheran Church 14 years ago, Diane Blahauvietz had come to care deeply about the community. She loved the closeness of the residents, and how, when the dark days came, people reached out to comfort one another. She felt honored to serve the people of Siren.

She was especially proud of her beloved Bethany. In the past five years, the congregation had grown by 150 members to nearly 700. It seemed some activity was always going on. As a result, members had embarked on an ambitious project to renovate and expand the church. From late November of last year until April while the church was torn apart, parishioners had worshipped each Sunday at Siren's school. Finally, in June, the project was pretty much wrapped up, after 2 years of hard work. "It was wonderful," Pastor Blahauvietz thought. "People were excited to be back home."

The night of the tornado, the 56 year old was standing in the kitchen of her Siren home, waiting for her husband, Larry, to come down from upstairs. The weather felt kind of spooky. She thought about going to the basement.

Larry had just returned from a fishing trip in Canada about two hours before and was busy unpacking. The 57 year old was just weeks away from retirement, and in April had been elected to take on the job of village president. He loved serving the community. He felt that in a small village like Siren, it would be a part-time position he could handle without a lot of stress.

As the tornado tore through the north end of town, the Blahauvietzs were unaware of the destruction. On the south end, where they lived, there had just been high winds and hail. They never made it to the basement. As Pastor Diane looked out the window, she could see the trees swaying mightily and hear the hail hitting their house. It sounded as if they were being shot at. Larry and Pastor Diane were afraid the windows on the west side of the house would break, but they didn't.

And then the storm passed. The phone rang. It was their son, Scott, calling from Maple Grove, Minnesota. He had seen on Twin Cities television the tornado heading for Siren, and wanted to warn them. Scott's parents assured him they were fine. The yard was a mess and Pastor Diane could see a huge tree down at the neighbor's place. Otherwise it didn't seem too bad. Only hail and wind.

After she got off the phone, Pastor Diane and Larry went outside to talk to several of the McBrooms, who lived next door and were standing out in their yard. That's when they learned what had truly happened. Mika McBroom, 16, had been in the cooler at the new Dairy Queen on the other side of town. She looked at the pastor and said, "Pastor Diane, Siren is gone." Her account of what had happened left Pastor Diane cold. She needed to go to her church, her dear Bethany.

Larry and Diane hurried "downtown." Even in the darkness it was a horrific sight. Buildings and homes blown to pieces. Rescue vehicles everywhere. "Once we got downtown and saw all the emergency vehicles lined up along Highway 35, that is when it really hit that it wasn't just a little wind and hail," Larry would say later. But there, with destruction on all sides, stood Bethany Lutheran Church. "Thank God," Pastor Diane thought, in total amazement. "When a cement block building behind you is nowhere to be seen and your church is still standing there, it's awesome." The two carefully went inside the church through the broken doors. There was glass and debris all over; windows were broken; doors were blown off their frames. But running all the time through the pastor's mind, the church was still standing, these minor things could be fixed.

As she ventured back outside, Pastor Diane saw the most beautiful sight: The highway in front of the church was lined with emergency vehicles from all over—there to help. Atop the church stood a cross that was supposed to light up in the dark. Due to an architectural miscalculation, however, that had never happened—until the night of the tornado. That night, all the flashing lights from all the emergency vehicles shined like a beacon on the cross. To Pastor Diane, it was a message from God. Amidst the rubble, she thought, God was telling the people of Siren: "I'm still here." The presence of Bethany Lutheran Church and, as it would turn out, all the other churches in town, gave hope to a great number of people. Hope that many would need in the difficult days to come.

After spending half an hour at the church, Pastor Diane and Larry went up to the emergency operation center, and witnessed the chaos there. Pastor Diane stood and talked to people. Her presence there an important comfort for many. "People just came up to me and would simply say I am okay—almost like checking in," Pastor Diane said. "I think that night the people that were there were just kind of shell-shocked. People just coming up and saying, 'I need a hug.'" Pastor Diane and Larry stayed there until midnight, and then went home to get some rest. They knew the days to come would be long ones.

But just an hour later at 1 A.M., Siren Police Chief Dean Roland showed up at their home and said Larry needed to go back downtown. As village president, Larry had to declare a state of emergency in Siren. "That was an emotional moment for me," Larry would later say. "It was an indication of the challenging days to come and the seriousness of the disaster." The next day, he presided over an emergency meeting of the village board, the first of many to come in the next few days and weeks. They decided to hire an experienced disaster team from Hugo, Minnesota, to handle cleaning up public property. Residents were also allowed to put their debris out near the street, and the Krieger crews would haul it away for free.

Given the utter destruction, county and state emergency management crews decided to institute a curfew, and seal off the village. Going in and out required a pass. It was an effort to cut down on the amount of traffic heading through town and to prevent looting. It was, for the most part, successful. Larry was also busy helping coordinate efforts with the numerous federal and state agencies that had descended on the area to provide disaster relief. Larry, like many others in Siren, discovered during those difficult days that he is a strong person, able to rise up in the face of adversity. "I have learned that I have the ability to cope under stress," he said.

Humor in the face of adversity became a way to help cope with the difficult days after the tornado. Village Attorney George Benson commented, tongue-in-cheek, to Larry one day, "Bob Lee was president of the village for eight years, and it grew and prospered. You're in office for two months, and the village is a disaster."

Due to the loss of power and phone service after the storm, people from outside the area were frantic. Pastor Diane was truly amazed at how many people drove to Siren the next day from as far away as the Twin Cities—to make sure she was okay and to check out Bethany. Once assured, they left. Thousands also poured into Siren to help with the clean up. Bethany's new parking lot, barely two weeks old at the time, became a drop-off/pick-up site for the volunteers. When visitors arrived into town, one of the first things they saw was the message on the sign in front of the church. A member

had put it up. It read, "We are here. God is here. We are blessed."

"We wanted all of those wonderful volunteers to know the Siren Spirit may have been broken but was not defeated," Pastor Diane said.

Siren was not defeated. Within hours of the tornado, a massive effort to pick up the pieces and put the puzzle back together again was well underway. And as residents cleaned up, they found items that they were sure signified God's presence.

One Bethany Lutheran Church member—an older lady named Francis England, who had lost a dear friend and then her husband, Moe, all within a year—lost part of her home in the tornado. As they were cleaning up at her house, they found a porcelain angel that had hung in her bedroom, which had been destroyed. The angel was on the lawn, in perfect condition.

Shortly after the storm, Siren resident Barb Lyga was helping with brush removal at an apartment building in town. There, under a pile of branches, she caught sight of something sparkling in the grass. When she bent over to pick it up, she discovered it was an angel pin. "To me it was some sort of 'sign,'" Lyga said, "with a message that we are being watched over throughout this disturbance in our area."

Pastor Diane had a beautiful ceramic plate in a stand on her desk. The word "BELIEVE" was painted on it. Most everything was blown off her desk, but that word never moved.

How could the faithful not believe? While the tornado wreaked havoc on the community, it also taught residents some valuable lessons. "Many people have a new appreciation for life and what really is important," Pastor Diane says, reflecting on the silver lining that came with the dark storm clouds. "We have seen the very best of people in their willingness to reach out and help us. We have received gifts of money, quilt donations; offers to help from so many from across the United States. We have the opportunity to rebuild and start anew. Siren will recover and will not only be a 'good-looking' town, but a stronger community. It will take time, but there is hope in the air . . . and God is still here!"

A Final Farewell

"It was like losing an old friend."

—*Siren Resident Jamie Mier, talking about his destroyed home*

By Barb Lyga

Jamie Mier lived at Birchview Group Home, a residence for adult men with developmental disabilities, for 15 years before he was able to purchase his own home in Siren in 1994. It was a giant step toward independence—a new life on his own. The tornado's winds changed all that, sweeping through his home, blowing away that independence he so treasured. His house was torn down in July, too heavily damaged to be repaired.

He went bowling in Frederic, south of Siren, the night of the tornado, and heard about a tornado warning while he was there. The power went out while they were bowling and the games were cancelled. The sky was yellow in Frederic. Police officers wouldn't allow them to go into Siren. There were heavy rains when they set off on foot, walking north on the Gandy Dancer Trail, which went right into Siren. Trees were down across the trail.

When Jamie finally got into town, he went to the Pheasant Inn, a bar and restaurant in the center of Siren, where he learned that he and the others he was with could spend the night at the high school. He couldn't go into his home because of all the wires and power lines that were down. Jamie helped set up cots in the gym. He stayed awake all night there with his friends. They waited for the sun to rise and then went back to check on his house. It was then that the devastation hit him. His cat was nowhere to be found.

His house was a mess. The sink was dislodged. Water was running from the pipes. Doors off the hinges. Windows gone. Glass all over everything. Curtains blown out the open windows. Many volunteers came by to help him clean out the house. WCCO Channel 4 News interviewed Jamie as he sat on the back porch of his house. He appeared on the 5:00 P.M. news on June 21st.

All Jamie's electrical equipment was untouched. These are the most important items to Jamie; the things he would be lost without. Jamie loves karaoke and recording his own songs. It's the focus of his life. Jamie took his video camera and recorded the demolition of his home. "It was like losing an old friend," he said.

Had Jamie been home the night of the

tornado, it's likely he wouldn't have found a safe place. His home had no basement. He may not have survived.

Jamie offers these words of wisdom about what happened: "Don't fool with Mother Nature because you never know what you'll get."

Sharing Shelter

"The woodchucks snuggled right up against him and watched the crawlspace entrance."

—Siren Resident Darren Lund, recounting a story told to him by a tornado survivor

By Darren Lund

I got up to Siren around four in the afternoon the day after the storm. After getting checked in with the Red Cross, I was on my way to my Uncle Gene Lund's house down where the Auto Stop used to stand on the north end of town. On my way, I saw many familiar faces and had to stop. One man I encountered told me quite an unusual story.

As I helped him move debris, he told me that he and his wife were outside when the storm hit, so they took cover by crawling under their house because they had no basement. Right before the tornado hit, he saw two rather large woodchucks run from his shed and into the crawlspace where he and his wife were sheltered. Being very surprised and afraid at the same time, the man didn't make a sound. The woodchucks snuggled right up against him and watched the crawlspace entrance. When the storm was over, the woodchucks walked out of the crawlspace, looked back at the man and his wife and then were on their way.

I found this very interesting since humans and woodland creatures tend to avoid each other. But when a storm is about to strike and man and creature alike are looking for shelter, I guess all are friends.

The Intensity

"The tornado's suction made you feel like you would be slammed into the floorboards above."

—*Laura Fossum, Siren Resident*

By Barb Lyga

Laura Fossum's family lived in a nice home, right in the village of Siren.

She and her husband, Darrel, spent 16 years improving their house—building an addition, putting on a deck. Their yard had two sheds, a dog pen, lots of plants, bushes, lilacs, roses and peonies. Darrel and Laura's two children—Bobbi Jean and Justin, now 19 and 15—had grown up there.

The town was home for the Fossums. Laura liked living in a small community where she knew her neighbors. All around, a nice place to live she thought.

Just before the storm hit, Laura was at home with Darrel. They received a phone call warning them a twister was bearing down on Siren. They got into their 2-foot crawl space just in time. The tornado sounded like being inside of a large vacuum cleaner with a very deep, loud motor. "We're not going to make it out alive," a petrified Laura thought. She could hear boards breaking above them, twisting back and forth. Everything was moving around in the house. "The tornado's suction made you feel like you would be slammed into the floorboards above," Laura would later recall.

After the storm passed, emerging from the safety of her crawl space, Laura saw a scene of total devastation. Her house was completely destroyed. The walls were bowed. Everywhere she looked, things were smashed, trees stripped or toppled, power lines littered the ground. The gas smell was strong. And there were so many gas leaks, it sounded like huge snakes. The whole scene was shocking—unreal, but yet real. Laura and a neighbor walked all around checking on other people.

Meantime, that night their son, Justin, was at his aunt, Lisa Otto's home, a few miles northeast of Siren. Lisa was desperately trying to find out what had happened to Laura and Darrel. At one point she was on the phone, and from the reports she was hearing blurted out, "We don't think Laura and Darrel made it." Justin overheard this and panicked. A single tear rolled down his face. Later that night Justin would have an emotional reunion with his parents. But for the next 3-4 weeks, he remained in a "zombie-like" state.

The day after the tornado, Laura thought, was like being in a horror movie. People were everywhere: cutting, trying to save whatever they could, and putting the rest into sorted piles of brush, metal, glass, garbage, appliances, etc. As the Fossums went through their belongings, they were able to salvage a number of items, such as their couch and some of their other furniture. Laura thinks that may be because the windows were open during the tornado. Perhaps, she reasons, the wind to some degree swept through the house, instead of building pressure on it (if the windows had been closed) causing it to explode.

While there was a lot of despair after the storm, there were good moments, too. Many acts of kindness, like the home offered to Laura and her family. Friends of the Fossum's daughter, Bobbi Jo, had called their parents in Hudson and told them the Fossums had no place to stay. Bruce and Jackie Nerby had a cabin near Siren and told the Fossums to go live there. "Wow, that is quite a generous offer," Laura thought.

She cried when she heard about it. The Fossums did stay there for a while. When they tried to give some rent money, the Nerbys refused, telling them just to pay the utilities.

Today, Laura still feels a sense of fear whenever there is storm. She misses all the trees. The once shady town, now has the sun beating right down on it. But much good has come from the tornado as well. There's a new feeling in town, Laura says. Residents are bonded with one another and share a closeness that comes only through experiencing such a tragedy together. People have shown how much they care.

Laura copes day-by-day, suffering from terrible migraine headaches. She most misses being able to have a place to call home. That will hopefully change soon, when her family's new pre-built home arrives. She has also learned to be more appreciative of family and friends. They are all that really matter. Someone was watching over Siren that night, she says, or many more lives would have been lost.

The Timbers Theatre sustained heavy damage, including roof damage. Seventy-five people were in the theater when the tornado struck. No one was injured, but the vehicles in the parking lot were turned over and tossed about. Photo courtesy of Inter-County Leader.

A Long Way Home

"The willingness to help each other will get the town rebuilt."

—Stephanie Whiteside, Siren Resident

By Luanne Swanson

Stephanie Whiteside has lived in Siren all of her life. The night of the tornado, the 23-year-old had attended a girls' softball game at the Siren ballpark. Later, after the game was called because of the approaching storm, Stephanie and her friend, Matt, decided to go to an 8:20 P.M. showing of the movie "Shrek" at Siren's Timbers Theatre. They arrived early, approximately 7:50 P.M., and while purchasing their tickets were told to go to their seats because of a possible tornado heading towards Siren. Stephanie figured the manager wanted the patrons in a secure area in case of an emergency.

They went and sat down as directed, and at 8:10 the previews began. Seated in the theatre were Stephanie, Matt and two other people. At 8:15 the electricity went out and a theatre employee came in and told them a tornado was near Grantsburg, 15 miles west of Siren, and that they should get down onto the floor on the ramp just inside the show room. The employee then shut the door, and, as pressure began to build, Stephanie's ears began to pop, reminding her of being in an airplane. She didn't hear the "freight train" sound often as-

sociated with a tornado, but surmised that she couldn't hear the sound because she was in a soundproof room.

Then, suddenly, there was the crashing sound of glass breaking. "It's here," she thought. Both the exit door located behind them and the door into the main part of the theatre blew open, but before she could react to the breaking glass, it was over. Everything went still.

The theatre's management asked everyone to remain where they were until they could assess the situation. After determining no one was injured, and that it was safe to go outside, they began to move towards the doors. Once outside, Stephanie saw a scene that she could only describe as a "wreckage yard." All the cars in the parking lot were damaged in some way. Hers was totaled. Looking around at the damage she was reminded of the phrase she had so often heard as a kid, "It looks like a tornado hit your bedroom."

After checking her car, Stephanie and Matt walked toward town to check on friends working at Auto Stop, a nearby convenience store.

Approaching the building and seeing the total devastation, she was relieved to learn her friends were safe. Continuing on to Kris' Pheasant Inn, they borrowed a friend's truck and headed out of town towards the west to check on people Matt was concerned about. After finding out everyone there was okay, Stephanie and Matt tried to return to Siren, but were stopped by deputies and rerouted around the village. They went down some back roads instead, trying to reach Stephanie's house to make sure her dad and brother were safe.

But with so many trees down, Stephanie became confused as to where exactly they were. And then eventually they had to stop driving because trees completely blocked the road. Determined though to continue, they abandoned the truck and started to walk, climbing over downed trees, through branches and debris for approximately a mile. Suddenly they saw a light, apparently from a flashlight and Stephanie yelled, hoping whoever it was would help her in her attempt to reach home. As the light came closer, she was relieved to see the familiar face of her neighbor, John Schmidt. She told John she was concerned about her family and needed to get home; John offered to take her there in his four-wheel drive truck. Finally reaching home, after what seemed to be the longest night of her life, Stephanie was relieved to find her dad and brother safe.

After seeing first-hand the destruction of much of the town that night, Stephanie knew there was much hard work ahead for everyone. But now, several months after the tornado, she is also certain the town will recover. "Siren is a small town but strong in the fact that everyone seems to know each other," Stephanie said. "The willingness to help each other will get the town rebuilt."

God is Great

"The power of God's love is so much greater than anything nature, or the kingdom of darkness can dish out. God will always have the last word, and it will be a good one."

—Mark Swenson, Siren Covenant Church Pastor

By Nancy Daniels

Mark Swenson and his family had just recently moved to Siren. Mark was the new pastor at Siren Covenant Church. In the few months since moving to Siren he had come to see the town as a place with a progressive spirit. A fairly close-knit community, but one not closed to outsiders.

Mark was also a carpenter. On the day of the tornado, he was busy working on his yet-to-be-completed home in the Lofty Pines development across from the water tower, on the southern side of the village. The weather was hot and humid, he thought, but didn't seem at all threatening. About an hour before the tornado hit, one of the neighbor children, Jessica Lysdahl, came over to ask if her family could come to their basement if the weather got bad. Their home was just to the south of Mark's. He said "sure" and continued working. He was passionate about finishing his "dream home." He had begun building it in December, almost completely by himself, from the ground up. All he could think about was getting it done, so he and his family could move in.

About 45 minutes later, Jessica, her two brothers, Jordan and Dillon, and her dad, Glen Lysdahl, came over because they had been listening to the weather and had lost power. It was through his neighbors that Mark learned the weather was taking a turn for the worse.

He was more irritated than concerned about the power going out. Now he could not work on the house. When the storm hit, he was looking out his garage door. The trees started to bend at a 45-degree angle. The wind started to pick up and he could hear what sounded like a huge train. It seemed as if at any moment, things would start flying. He wasn't even going to get his house done, he thought, before it was ripped apart. The wind lasted about 2-5 minutes. After the sound dissipated and the wind died down, there was some hail and heavy rain. Much to his amazement, his house had come through without a scratch.

After the storm, he ran into his friend and Siren resident, Dayton Daniels. Dayton asked him if he had a chainsaw. When he said he didn't but wanted to help, Dayton found him one and away they went. They headed first to Camp Ojibway, a few miles west of Siren, to

97

open the road. They worked for hours clearing trees to the camp. Later he went into town and saw the devastation there for the first time. It was overwhelming. He just couldn't believe how much damage the storm had caused. He helped out where he could, cutting brush and trees with his borrowed chainsaw. He finally went home between 2:00 and 3:00 A.M.

First thing early the next morning, he went out and bought his own chainsaw, so he could continue to help with the clean up. He first went to Paul and Laurie Riemer's house, a couple from his congregation. They lived on 4th Avenue and Works Progress Street, a block east of the Auto Stop, on the north end of town. Their home had been in the direct path of the tornado. Paul and Laurie had been trapped in their house for a few hours after the tornado had gone through. They were both very shaken, but unhurt and grateful to be alive. Mark cut trees there most of the morning and afternoon. He then went to Gerry and Gail Potvins, who live near Alpha, a small unincorporated town west of Siren about 10 miles. The tornado first touched down in the Alpha area. They lost most of their trees and their home was severely damaged. They had returned from a trip to the Twin Cities just hours after the tornado ripped through their property. Mark cleared trees there until dark. Many other volunteers also came to help the Potvins. One, a man named Gerry, just showed up with his skid steer. He stayed for two days. It was a real blessing, Mark thought.

Mark said of all of the volunteers he encountered: "They loved us. They blessed us, and helped us pick up the pieces. Their faces and love will never be forgotten."

He also gives thanks for what God has done in the community since the storm. "The power of God's love is so much greater than anything nature, or the kingdom of darkness can dish out," he said. "God will always have the last word, and it will be a good one."

A Modern Day Miracle

"They were preparing for 200 fatalities. Getting body bags and sites ready."

—*Dayton Daniels, Siren Volunteer Firefighter*

By Joan Daniels, Nancy Daniels and Chad Thomas

Among the many families to put down roots early in the Siren community were the Daniels; the family came to America from Sweden in the latter part of the 19th Century, helping found what would later become the Siren Covenant Church. Daniels Township west of Siren is named for the family.

Among the many descendants to remain in the area, Don Daniels, a grandson of the original family members who came to the United States. Don and his wife Joan have always lived in this rural community, raising four sons in Siren. They run a successful business, Daniels Plumbing and Heating—where two of their boys still work, David and Dayton. They like being close to their grandchildren, and attending their activities. That's exactly what they were doing early that hot and humid evening the tornado hit.

Don and Joan were at 14-year-old granddaughter Dayna Daniels' softball game. Dayna's dad, Dayton, was there as well. It was Dayton who told everyone of the approaching storm. Dayton, a volunteer firefighter, heard an early storm warning for Siren on his pager. After talking to one of the coaches, they decided to call the game at 7:30 P.M., so the visiting team could head home.

Dayton jumped in his truck for home, four miles southwest of Siren. It had been a long day, and the evening, hot and stuffy. He was looking forward to getting inside, with air conditioning. His wife, Nancy, and youngest daughter, Courtney, were close behind in another vehicle. Dayna went to a friend's house. By the time he got home, there were tornado warnings for Siren on television. The sky was dark and very close to the ground.

Don and Joan Daniels also headed for home. They were staying in their motor home at the time, while their new house was being built. The motor home was just a mile from the ball field, behind their plumbing store on the main highway running through town. By the time they got there, the low clouds were already rolling across the sky and there was constant thunder. But Don and Joan lingered outside, filling the water tank for their motor home before going inside and turning on the television. Storm warnings were scrolling across the bottom of the screen for several minutes, and then the power went out. It was still fairly light outside, and the Daniels remained largely unconcerned.

They were sitting in the motor home reading the paper when a knock came at their door. It was Susan Roy, who attended the same Siren church as the Daniels. Susan told them she had just been west of town, and that the weather conditions were much worse there. While Susan lived out in that direction, she thought it was too dangerous to go home in the approaching storm, and suggested the three of them all take shelter in their church's basement across the street.

By now, the clouds were moving faster and the thunder getting louder. Deciding the church might be too far, the three instead made a mad dash for the Daniels' plumbing store next to the motor home. They were only in the store a few minutes before the tornado's full fury bore down on them. Joan had previously opened the shades on the store's front window, and Don now stood there, looking out in disbelief. Debris was swirling all around, first to the north, then to the south. The sign on the bank across the street shook like a giant baby's rattle.

Joan and Susan crouched behind the store's counter. Joan would pop her head up every now and then and look out. Even without a direct view of the storm, she could hear it was bad. Things kept landing with a large thump on the building's roof. The tornado itself roared through like a freight train. Joan could feel the pressure building in her ears. Susan, a devoutly religious woman, prayed. Then it was gone.

During the tornado, The Daniel's son, Dayton, was home, huddled in the back bathroom with his family. It wasn't as bad there. They

were further away from the tornado's direct path. There was a constant low rumble of thunder and it got windy, but it rained just a little. Dayton kept checking outside. After a couple of minutes it seemed to be all over. The power went out but the phones were still working. Dayton and his wife, Nancy, called and checked on their daughter, Dayna. She was fine as well. Then Dayton got another call on his pager. (The first had warned them when they were at the ballpark of the approaching storm.) This one said Camp Ojibway, a church camp on the northeast end of Mud Hen Lake (six miles west of Siren), had been hit by the tornado, and that there were a lot of injuries. "Of course your worst fears run through your mind," Dayton would later recall. He took off immediately to help.

There was no direct way to get there. "There were major power lines down, pretty much wrecked on the highway," Dayton said. Trees covered the roads, forcing them to drive through the ditches. He stopped and asked Mark Swenson, the pastor at the Siren Covenant Church, to go with him and help. He also called his brother, David, to come with more heavy equipment. They had to work slowly. They had no idea if the power lines down on the road were dead or alive. After an hour and a half, they finally made it out to Camp Ojibway. None of the kids at the camp had serious injuries. "Relief," Dayton thought. "Just plain relief."

He spent most of the rest of the night clearing trees from North Mud Hen Lake Road with his bulldozer so that emergency vehicles could pass through.

Immediately after the storm, as Joan and Don Daniels, along with their friend, Susan

Roy, ventured out from the plumbing store. The first thing they noticed was that a big oak tree had fallen just across the street behind their church. But the church itself was okay. Miraculously, as the night wore on, Siren residents would learn all the other churches in town had also made it through the twister unscathed.

When they went around to the back of the building to their motor home, they discovered what had caused much of the racket they heard during the tornado. There, the rafters from the business next door, Lee's Sport and Saw, were scattered all over, including right through the Daniels' motor home. A cinder block had also blown through the window and was sitting on the dashboard. The back window was broken, and all the bed covers blown off. Glass was everywhere. The motor home was a loss. Four of their company vehicles were also badly damaged, as was the roof of their business.

That night they worried little, however, about their own loss. After emergency crews told them a shelter was being set up at the town's school, they headed right up there. Not to take any assistance, but to help. A young couple had given them a bag of towels and blankets. They took those supplies up there, too. Susan Roy was still with the Daniels. The three of them stayed at the school until 2 A.M., making sandwiches and comforting people. Then they went back to their store, sleeping on the floor.

The next morning, Joan, a lifelong Siren resident, walked around to see what was left of her little town. The furniture store was destroyed. Many years ago it had been the Siren Town Hall. Joan thought about going there as a kid on Saturday nights to watch Gene Autry and Roy Rogers films. In the winter, students had played basketball games there. In the summer, they had used the building as a roller rink. It had also served as the location for class plays, graduation ceremonies, dances and Memorial Day programs. Joan, and many other Siren residents, had fond memories of the building where they had spent much of their youth. Joan also soon discovered the home she had spent her teen-age years in was destroyed. It was too much for Joan to bear. Tears now streamed down her face.

There wasn't much time to ponder those losses. Grimly, there was a lot more devastation for Joan and the others to see. Among the other businesses destroyed, the old Siren Hotel; the Pour House, a popular restaurant and bar; the new Dairy Queen; a meat shop; the drug store; the chiropractic office; a convenience store; a mini mall; a bait shop. All important pieces of the Siren community. All blown apart in a matter of minutes.

The day after the tornado, Dayton, the Daniels' son, was very tired. He hadn't slept since the previous morning. But he continued clearing trees from driveways, and spent about 8 hours clearing trees from Clam Lake Drive, four miles east of Siren. Dayton was running on adrenaline. "There's no way physically that you'd be able to do that," Dayton says, "without just *having* to do that." The day was so surreal. It was hard to believe the town had actually been in the path of such devastation and there were only 3 fatalities. "I've talked to people in the emergency business," Dayton said. "They were preparing for 200 fatalities. Getting body bags and sites ready."

Truly, Dayton thought, this was a modern-day miracle.

The Search

"As we got into the cooler, you could hear things slam against the building. The only thing I could think of was, 'where was my son?'"

—Becky Lamphere, Siren Area Resident

By Chad Thomas and Wendy Morris

The night of the tornado, Siren coach and teacher Ryan Karsten was at the Siren ball field, coaching a girls' softball game. At 7:30 P.M. he called the game early, after getting reports that a bad storm was headed their way. (This was the game Dayton Daniels' daughter had been playing in.) It was a little out of character for the extremely competitive coach to do that, especially given that the game was only in the fifth inning with the score tied. Karsten would later say he had a funny feeling that night about the storm that he just couldn't shake.

As soon as the game ended, players from the opposing team boarded a bus for Shell Lake, 25 miles east of Siren. The Siren girls also dispersed and headed for home. Karsten, along with fellow coach, Chad Gibson, and a student, stayed a little longer at the ball field to pick up. As they finished, the skies darkened, and Karsten's concerns increased. Remembering 15 students were in the school lifting weights, he headed up there to tell them to go home as well. On his way, he heard on the radio that the situation had become more precarious—the severe thunderstorm warning was now a tornado warning.

As he arrived at the school, Siren resident Sharon D'Jock pulled in just behind him, and agreed to take some of the students home. The others were told to call their parents to come and get them. Karsten then left briefly to check on a student who was supposed to be out jogging on the school's track. When he got there, he discovered she had already left. Karsten returned to the school, finding six students still needed a ride. Another parent who showed up at this time said she'd take three of them home. Karsten agreed to take the others.

Karsten was able to quickly drop off two of the students, leaving the 26-year-old with freshman Cody Lamphere. Karsten could see the storm coming in. The sky was white, but the town totally black. Everything was absolutely still. As Karsten drove through town to take Cody home, they saw many people standing outside their homes looking in the direction of the storm. As they continued on, two baseball-size pieces of hail struck Karsten's truck, prompting Karsten to head for his house to wait out the storm. He figured they'd call Cody's mom, Becky Lamphere, and tell her where he was once they got there. But at Karsten's apartment, they learned Becky was searching for her 14-year-old son, so they ventured back out to find her.

Becky had left just after 8 P.M. to pick up Cody, a little earlier than normal. While the sky was looking a little ominous, she had actually gone to town early because the fish were biting that evening, and figured Cody would want to get in a few casts before it got dark. When she arrived at the school, however, no one was there. She didn't know it at the time, but Cody, of course, was with Karsten. She checked the baseball field. No one there either. She went back to the school. Still no Cody. Becky decided to go to the Holiday gas station to use a pay phone to call her parents. They told her Cody was with Karsten, and urged her, "Get inside now."

But the doors to the store were locked, and Becky didn't think it was that bad. So she stood behind the rock pillars at the entrance of the store, figuring she would wait out the storm there.

Assistant Store Manager Debbie Pohlkamp was just on her way into the store's pop cooler when Becky came pounding on the door. Unlike Becky, Pohlkamp had already seen the tornado coming, and knew it was bad. "It was huge," Pohlkamp said. She didn't think twice about going to help Becky, figuring that if Becky stayed outside in all the flying debris, she'd be killed. So Pohlkamp ran to another door, opened it and screamed to Becky. The wind was so strong Pohlkamp had to pull Becky into the store. As she tried to close the door, Pohlkamp almost went flying outside herself.

Together, Pohlkamp and Becky made their way to the cooler—joining four other store employees, 15 customers and someone's dog—to ride out the twister. "As we got into the cooler, you could hear things slam against the building," Becky said. "The only thing I could think of was where was my son."

Her son was just a few blocks away, himself struggling to get out of the tornado's path. After they had left Karsten's apartment, Cody and his teacher had gone back to the school. Not finding Becky there, they left, heading for Auto Stop, another convenience store in town. They planned to ride out the storm under Auto Stop's overhang. (If they had made it to Auto Stop, there's a strong possibility they would have been killed. The store and overhang, in the direct path of the tornado, were ripped apart. The only thing left standing was the restroom where people inside the store had taken cover.) By this time the tornado's full force was bearing down on Siren. As Cody and his teacher drove in front of the school, trees and pieces of buildings began to fly past. Karsten knew they had to take cover fast. Initially though a big gust of wind caught his Ford Explorer and he was unable to turn the vehicle into the school's parking lot; the wind was just too powerful. But eventually he somehow managed to pull into the lot, and he and Cody made a mad dash for the school. In the strong wind, both of them had to heave on the door to get it open. Once they did, Karsten grabbed Cody and threw him into the school. The two then made their way further into the building, riding out the remainder of the storm in a safer location.

After the tornado passed, Karsten headed outside, and checked on another teacher's car in the south parking lot of the school. From what he could first see, he thought, the storm hadn't been too bad. But it didn't take Karsten long to realize that initial assessment was very wrong. While the area to the south of the school wasn't badly damaged, when he looked out some windows on the north side of the building, he saw an entirely different scene. In short, Siren had been blown away. The 26-year-old sprang into action, leaving Cody at the school and heading out into the village to check on people.

When Becky emerged from the cooler, she scanned the town. Pohlkamp pointed out to Becky that eight, twelve-packs of pop had slammed into the area where she had been standing, and part of the roof had collapsed there as well. Becky also noticed all the windows in her new car were gone. Smashed by the storm's fury. "I have never in my life ever been in anything so horrible," Becky would recall later. But at that moment, all the destruction was of little concern. Becky still had to find Cody. She quickly scribbled a note, put it on the car saying she was headed for the school and took off running.

She was not more than two blocks from the gas station when she heard Karsten yelling at her from the other direction. His loud booming voice had always made Becky laugh. That night he yelled to her amidst the rubble, "I've got him. I've got him. Cody's okay." It made Becky begin weeping, but yet she was laughing, too. "God that voice," she said, "it was the greatest sound that I had ever heard."

Karsten could see the initial shock on Becky's face. Her eyes were as big as saucers. She gave Karsten a big hug. "I felt joy that I could at least ease her pain a little bit," Karsten said. He ran back to the school and got Cody. A short time later mother and son were finally reunited. "They say there are a lot of heroes," Becky says, "Karsten is right up there with me."

In the darkness that night there would be many more emotional reunions for Siren residents. And many more heroes to emerge.

The Night The Walls Shook

"As the three headed for the bathroom, Marti, in the rear, felt the spatter of glass on the back of his calves from broken windows caused by flying debris outside and the pressure of the vacuum the funnel had created."

—*Robert Heinze, Regional Housing Manager for Catholic Charities Bureau*

By Robert Heinze

At 8:20 P.M. the night of Monday, June 18, the kind of thing nightmares are made of became reality for the people of the Village of Siren in northwestern Wisconsin—a killer tornado. Among the buildings lying in the tornado's approximately mile-wide path was Lakewood Apartments, a five-unit apartment building for persons with developmental disabilities owned by Catholic Charities Bureau of Superior.

The air was heavy that night. Steel doors and windows were coated with a film of steam from the humidity. There was no indication of what forces would bear down on the people and landscape in the 30-mile path from Alpha in Burnett County to Spooner in Washburn County.

Only minutes before the tornado struck, a warning flashed across the television screen inside Lakewood Apartments signaling Marti Buskirk and his grandfather, Dwight "Dutch" Taylor that danger could be headed their way. They were watching wrestling, but had no idea of the "battle royal" they would have to face themselves.

As they were considering the need for action, fellow tenant, Dan McDowell, came to the door. He had been listening to a police scanner and realized the danger they were in. There was precious little time to ponder after Dan's arrival. As the three headed for the bathroom, Marti, in the rear, felt the spatter of glass on the back of his calves from broken windows caused by flying debris outside and the pressure of the vacuum the funnel had created.

The three crowded into the bathtub for the next few moments, the small room became like the inside of a vacuum cleaner bag. The walls shook, the floor and sides of the tub vibrated and the trio's ears were filled with the tell-tale sound of a freight train, as they seemingly laid on the tracks beneath one.

When the terror ended, the three emerged from the bathroom with flashlights they had grabbed to find every window in Marti's apartment broken. One window frame was pushed into the room. The whole north wall of the apartment was pulled away from the rest of the room by about an inch and a half.

Following directly behind the tornado was torrential rain. With half of the shingles being ripped off the roof and some holes in the sheathing, the rain had easy access to the attic. As it accumulated, streams began to follow the path of least resistance and fill the globes in the apartment light fixtures. As the globes grew heavy with water, they began crashing to the already glass strewn and rain soaked floors.

Outside the tenants found a surreal, twisted mass of downed trees and power lines. Building and household debris were everywhere. Blown insulation, sucked out of the Lakewood attic and mixed with the rain and tree leaves, coated everything outside like an old fashioned "tar and feathering." But for flashlight beams, darkness was everywhere. Any car sitting in the path of the storm invariably had broken windows, dents and a layer of furry insulation and tree leaves. The worst ones had taken a somersault.

The miracle of it all is that this storm claimed only two lives directly related to the action of the tornado itself and a third, indirectly.

Marti is living with his grandparents awaiting complete reconstruction of his apartment. Dan has returned to a group home he had just left on June 1, awaiting the chance to return to his new home.

Tenant Chris Potter, who took shelter in a closet in his apartment, had a 15-foot-long section of channel steel enter about six feet into his bedroom wall like a giant warhead. He is living with his parents in Shell Lake for the time being.

Sherry Welsh was not home when the tornado struck. She was able to return to her apartment after a week, as her apartment had only a broken window. Norma Kroll's apartment had some drywall cracking and she was able to remain in her apartment.

The overall damage estimate at Lakewood Apartments is in the $45,000 range. The project faired better than the average building in the neighborhood. Other homes and businesses on the same block, and nearby, were demolished.

The bleak landscape began to show signs of resurrection the very next day after the storm. The buzz of chainsaws could be heard everywhere in town; Joe Wacek, director of Diversified Services, Inc., another Catholic Charities affiliate, cleared away the trees, which had fallen closest to the building.

The day after that, a larger crew of volunteers appeared on the scene to pick up debris outside and broken glass inside, and continue removing downed trees. Roofers also arrived that day.

It will likely be early August before all the tenants are able to move back home. But, they are thankful that they were among the fortunate whose home still stands amidst the awesome devastation of this tornado.

Editors Note: This article originally appeared in the Catholic Charities Bureau's August Newsletter. It is reprinted in this book with the Bureau's permission, and that of the author. The tenants were able to move back into their homes the first weekend in August.

❧

Priorities Changed

"House cleaning is just not as important as it once was. I just spend a lot more time visiting and enjoying each day."

—*Rosie Howe, Siren Resident*

By Nancy Daniels

John Howe and Rosie Mitchell lived on Herman Johnson Road, just a couple of miles out of town on a beautiful hobby farm. They had lived together in this house for nearly three years. John and Rosie had a blended family. Rosie always referred to it as "his, mine and ours." Together, they had five daughters.

The night of the tornado, Rosie was planting flowers and John was working to take some old stain off the deck. John and Rosie had plenty to do; in less than two weeks, they were planning to unite their families permanently. They were getting married June 29, capped off by a big reception at their home.

In between the yard work the night of the tornado, they were grilling hamburgers. Jennifer, Rosie's oldest daughter, had just come home with a friend, Kelley Wampfler. They knew some kind of storm was headed their way, but didn't really think anything more of it. After supper, around 7:45, Rosie biked with the girls to take Kelley home. She lived just down the road from them. On the way back, Rosie wanted to keep biking a little farther and maybe go into town. Jennifer decided to turn into the driveway because she didn't like the sound of the thunder. Rosie kept going, but after she'd biked a little more than a mile, she got a feeling of panic and turned back to the house.

The four girls who lived with John and Rosie were all bathed and in their jammies by 8:00. John and Rosie were sitting on the porch when the wind started picking up. Rosie's sister-in-law, Carrie Moen, called to tell them a tornado was coming down Highway 70, just a few miles away. Rosie and John's house only had a small cellar under the kitchen. Rosie's mom, Darlene Baker, lived just down the road from them and had a full basement in the hobby farm she was renting.

Rosie felt this urgent need to get the girls out of there fast. John wanted to stay and get the hanging plants in first. Normally, Rosie would have waited for him, but she felt strongly that she had to leave right away. So with fears and mixed emotions, Rosie loaded the girls into the van and left.

John and Rosie Howe, with their family, on their wedding day.

Two minutes later they were at Rosie's mom's place. She was not aware of the weather situation. Together they grabbed a candle, some blankets and the phone, and headed for the basement. They called Annie Slater, a neighbor lady in her 60s who lived alone. They knew she was home, but she did not answer her phone, so they left the message telling her to get to a safe place.

The atmosphere in the basement was tense. The girls were crying and panicked. The power had gone off, and the candle wouldn't light. Once it finally did, they prayed and sang songs. Just as they were beginning to calm down, they heard something break up above them, and the basement door slammed shut. Seconds later, it was over.

Darlene was the first one out of the basement. There were trees down everywhere. There was a power pole on top of Rosie's van. The barn and other outbuildings were all gone. Then Rosie panicked, worrying about John. She tried to call but couldn't get through. Seconds later he came walking up, saying over and over again, "It's gone, it's gone, everything's gone." Then he shouted, "Get the kids out of the house!" He could hear gas hissing and there were power lines down. Everyone got out, but they were all in shock. No one knew what to do. A man no one recognized came walking up. He'd been in his car on the road during the storm and couldn't get through because of the downed trees.

They all seemed to be in a daze. Rosie

started walking down to her house, and began seeing stuff everywhere. Half of the house was gone. The barn and garage were gone. John's truck and large trailer were gone. Rosie walked back to check on their neighbor Annie Slater. (The one they had tried to call.) She wasn't thinking, because there were trees and power lines down everywhere. She had to jump over them to get down her driveway. Annie was okay. She had stayed under her stairway during the storm, just barely making it there from the shower before the tornado hit. She walked back to John and the kids. Emily's foot was bleeding.

Red and Joyce Anderson, and their son, Darwin, were the first ones there that night. They owned the house Rosie's mom was renting. John's Dad, Herb Howe, came shortly after that to get the family. John and Rosie had a 5th wheel camper for sale a few miles away on Highway 70. They thought they could stay in that for the night, and longer if necessary. Herb had to tell them that, along with their house, their camper was gone, too, so they stayed at John's folks' house that night.

The next morning, John and Rosie found their two horses wandering around by the home Rosie's mom rented. They caught them and walked them cross-country about one mile to their friends', Jeff and Kelly Alden, place, who kept the horses in their barn. John and Rosie then went back to their house to see what was left, and where they should start. There were already "tons" of friends and family there to help. The number of people who showed up was overwhelming. Without all the assistance, they could never have completed all they had to do.

A week and a half later, John and Rosie's wedding went off without a hitch. June 29th, they had a beautiful ceremony in Our Redeemer Lutheran Church in neighboring Webster. They moved the reception to the ballroom of the Lodge on Crooked Lake (a hotel on the north end of Siren). Rosie credits her friend, Kris Phernetton, for lining up the reception. Local stores donated most of the food. Kris' friends and relatives volunteered their time to serve and food and drinks. Despite all that had happened, it was a special night to remember.

Immediately after the tornado, John, Rosie and the girls lived at The Lodge, and then moved in with Rosie's sister, Julie Steiner, and her family in Webster. On August 4 they moved into a home they had been planning to buy before the tornado.

They feel so fortunate to finally have a place to call home again. Dealing with the aftermath of the tornado has been difficult on the girls, but they are feeling more secure day by day. They sleep more peacefully at night, and have to crawl into bed with mom and dad less often. For Rosie, since the tornado she has learned that she's a very strong person, and more spiritual than she ever thought. Her family means more to her than any of the things she lost. "House cleaning is just not as important as it once was," Rosie said. "I just spend a lot more time visiting and enjoying each day."

A Lesson in Kindness

"It was really great to see how people were willing to put their lives on hold to help others who were in need."

—Joe Cremin, Siren Resident

By Terry Mengel

At first, Joe Cremin didn't really know how destructive the tornado had been. While the 19-year-old lived about 15 miles east of Siren in one of the hardest hit areas, during the storm Joe was in Webster, north of Siren. Up there, hardly a branch was blown off a tree. His parents were away in Indiana, so he couldn't call them.

He quickly realized, however, the scope of the devastation as he tried to drive home that evening. So many trees and power lines had fallen on the roads, the closest Joe could get to his house was still a mile away.

He decided to walk. Joe couldn't believe it. It seemed every tree that possibly could have fallen on the driveway had. It took him 15 minutes to climb his way through the debris.

At Joe's house, the small third story, which was his dad's office, had blown completely off. It was laying upside down on their turn-around driveway. Thankfully, there was not too much more destruction to the house; just the trees that laid "EVERYWHERE!" It's an image Joe will not soon forget.

Friends began showing up immediately after that to help start cutting trees to get down the road and to the house. At any given time, there were 15 to 20 people working to clear the mess. "It was really great to see how people were willing to put their lives on hold," Joe said, "to help others who were in need."

A Plea for Mercy

"My God, oh my God, do not forsake us; don't let us survive the tornado to be burned alive in the basement!"

—*Robert Field, Tornado Survivor*

By Robert Field

June 18 started typically enough, a northwest Wisconsin summer morning: warm, with the promise of becoming hot in the afternoon. Throughout the afternoon and early evening the heat-generated thunderstorms developed and built. A guest, two big, white dogs and myself were relaxing in the living room, playing Yahtzee (not the dogs).

We were watching "The Weakest Link" on Twin Cities Channel 11, and saw the tornado watch turn to a tornado warning, with reports of a tornado on the ground near Grantsburg. As it became increasingly apparent that the tornado was headed our way we turned on the radio, and got the flashlights and radio ready to take to the basement. The radio station was tracking the tornado by the minute . . . Grantsburg, Alpha, Falun, due in Siren at 8:26 P.M.

We went to the basement, two men and two dogs, and waited for what we assumed would be a good meteorological show. We sat in the southwest corner of the basement on chairs. The basement lights were on. The radio station went off the air almost at the minute of the predicted arrival in Siren, and the basement

lights went off. We turned on the flashlights. We then knew that there was actually some kind of winds, and maybe this might be a really good show. We found another radio station from Pine City and were listening to that. Then we heard it . . . the Train, just like you'd always been told; it sounded like a freight train moving fast.

Within one-half minute of hearing the "train," the tornado struck in all its fury. It was black as a cave outside the basement windows, and the sound was so furious we could not hear one another, even by yelling. Instinctively we each laid on top of a dog, and covered our heads with our hands. The intensity of the wind continued to increase, and the thinking part of our brains told us that if it continued to increase, we would die. We had no way to know how much it would increase. Then the basement door blasted open, and the furious wind circled in the basement, throwing everything about and turning the air dark with dust. We could not see the light from the flashlights.

And then FIRE blasted in through the open door. We had had a daylong campfire in the fire pit, and the entire fire, embers, ashes, burning pine and oak logs, all flew into the basement, brightly inflamed by the wind and looking like it had shot out of a blowtorch. My God, oh my God, do not forsake us; don't let us survive the tornado to be burned alive in the basement.

But then the intensity of the wind decreased; the flames went out, and we thought we might live. And then we heard it. Couldn't believe it, but both heard it: a woman screaming. We ran up the stairs to look for whomever we had heard. When we got to the top we were not in the kitchen, but the open air; the house was gone from above us.

Again, the screaming. We called out: "Where are you?" And then we saw them, standing in the remains of what had once been my farmhouse: a woman was crazy-out-of-her-mind with fear and awe; the little girl, about four years old, was nearly catatonic. We held mother and child: stroked the girl's head. Safe. We're safe now. Everything's going to be alright. Safe. Safe. Alive.

They had been driving by in an SUV, trying to out-run the storm. A log crashed through the back window and landed on the seat. They saw the house. Maybe they have a basement. Safe. Safe. Alive. They had seen all of it; mother carrying child across the yard to the destroyed house, amidst the fury of the storm. Four cars and trucks were rolled across the yard. Trees and debris were flying everywhere—sure to kill anything it struck. And yet, they walked across the yard through it all, surely with the wings of an angel spread over them.

The storm then passed, hell-bent on continuing its terrifying, murderous path of destruction. We came out of the basement to a new world. The farm gone; the woods gone; only the mangled portion of the house that was above our heads remained. The four humans gathered in the yard gave thanks to God for sparing us. Strangers praying together amidst the chaos and ruin. Thank God. Thank God. We're alive. All we are is dust in the wind.

Tornado Takes Human Toll

"These are experiences which leave scars that may soften, but never heal."

—*Mary Adeline Boehm, June 12, 1899*
The New Richmond Cyclone

Photo courtesy of Star Tribune.

Tom Haseltine survived the tornado but lost his life when he hit a downed guy wire while on a four-wheeler trying to get to his brother, Lyle's, destroyed home, which was across the lake from the Scenic View Campground owned by Haseltine and his wife, Carol.

A Life Well-Lived

"He loved life, he loved people, and lived all of his 60 years without wasting a minute of it."

—Carol Haseltine, talking about her husband Tom

By Nancy Jappe

Tom Haseltine and his wife, Carol, were at their home on Poquette Lake the night of the tornado. That's where the two owned and ran the Scenic View Campground, just off Highway 70 on the eastern edge of Burnett County. They had their television on, and saw the warning that a storm was headed their way. But because of the trees surrounding the house and campground, they couldn't see what was coming from a distance. So Tom got into his truck and went out to the highway to keep tabs on the skies. He had a cell phone with him.

His brother, Lyle, called from his house across the lake with a warning about the storm, prompting Tom to head back to the campground to make sure the campers there were safe. He and Carol went down into the small space under their house to wait out the storm.

When they emerged from under the house a short time after the tornado had passed, they were thankful to see their house was intact. But as they looked out at the lake, they noticed Lyle's house was gone. Tom got on the four-wheeler and tried to take a shortcut through the woods, but couldn't get through. A tree had

fallen across the pickup, so he continued on the four-wheeler to the other side of the lake by way of the road. It was on that road, almost directly across from his house, that the four-wheeler ran into a downed guy wire, throwing Tom off the machine. It was about 9 P.M.

Tom's son, Dean, and his wife came to check on them right after the storm. After Carol told them Tom had gone to assist Lyle, they, too, went to lend a helping hand, but couldn't get through. There were downed trees everywhere. They could see a man lying dead in the road, but weren't close enough to identify him, and couldn't get any information on who he was.

They went back to the campground, told Carol about it, then tried another route to get to Lyle's place. This time, they made it. Dean called Carol on his cell phone to report that Lyle and his wife were okay, and that they were staying to help get a vehicle out. Carol assumed that "they" meant Tom was there too. When Dean and his wife stopped back later, however, she learned that they hadn't seen Tom at all.

Carol tried not to panic, but at this point she knew something was terribly wrong. Tom would check on his brother's safety before going to help anyone else. The hours dragged on, with no sign of Tom or word of his whereabouts.

In the meantime, seasonal campers from nearby towns came to check the damage to their campers. Carol signaled them to come into the house. She had just heard on the CB that the person who had been killed was "a guy on a four-wheeler, and that he owned the resort on the other side of the lake." Scenic View is the only resort on Poquette Lake. "I just about went crazy," Carol recalled later. "We called everywhere we could think of, law enforcement, the DNR, hospitals and mortuaries. No one would tell us anything."

At 4 A.M., seven hours after the accident, deputies came to the house and confirmed what Carol already knew was true: her husband had been that man on the four-wheeler. He had died instantly, after striking the downed wire.

Sixty-year-old Thomas Dean Haseltine was born in St. Paul, Minnesota, and lived the first part of his life in Rice Lake, Wisconsin. As a young man, he worked as the meat market manager at the National Tea Store in Spooner, Wisconsin, directly east of Siren. He later moved to Webster, where he owned and operated the IGA food store in the 1960s.

After moving back to Spooner in the early 1970s, Tom followed in his father's footsteps to become a skilled mason contractor, specializing in stone masonry. He did massive stone fireplaces and other rock work for many expensive homes in the area.

Tom joined Carol in managing the Scenic View Bar and Campground after they were married 11 years ago. Karaoke was one of the attractions at the campground bar, with Tom's rich, mellow voice a big part of it. Singing came naturally to him, as did many other talents.

"Tom could make, build or do anything; and if there wasn't a tool for the job, he would simply invent one," Carol said. "He had a quick wit and a wonderful sense of humor. He was famous for his bear hugs and belly laughs. He made a lasting impression on everyone he met. He loved life, he loved people, and lived all of his 60 years without wasting a minute of it."

Coping with Reality

"It was something out of a nightmare."

—*Pam Brown, Ruth Schultz's daughter*

By Nancy Jappe

The night of the tornado, Ruth Schultz, her husband, Ray, and son, Lenny Pfundheller, were at home playing cards. The phone rang. It was Ruth's daughter, Pam Brown, who lived nearby. She was calling to warn them of an approaching tornado. Ruth hung up and turned on her scanner. A few minutes later, Ruth called Pam back, saying she could see the funnel above the house. "We will be OK," Ruth told Pam. That was the last Pam heard from her mother.

As the tornado bore down on them, the three tried to take cover. Ruth had just made it to the top of the basement stairs when the tornado hit, blowing debris against her. After the storm passed, Lenny found his mother out on the lawn, pressed against a toilet from the bathroom. He begged his mother not to die. She said she wouldn't.

Pam looked outside her home, just a couple miles south of her mother and Ray's house. The sky was black, but it was not raining where Pam and her husband, Randy, were. They could see a purple wall over in the direction of Pam's mother's house. Pam tried to call Ruth, but the phone kept ringing and ringing. She and Randy thought Ruth and Ray were outside looking at the damage. They started over to check on the elderly couple, having to take alternate roads because of the downed trees.

"It was something out of a nightmare," Pam thought when she saw the damage at her mother's house. The home's walls were still standing, but all that was left of the kitchen paneling was one 6 x 6 piece that fit near the plug-in socket on the wall. Because this was an older house, with older-style paneling, the piece was easily recognizable. Pam's husband Randy had put a new roof on the house. He found pieces of roof in all different places. Pam and Randy thought it would be a miracle if anyone was alive. Ray was the first person they saw when they were able to get near the house. He didn't recognize them at first. "I am doing okay, but my wife is not doing good," Ray told them.

Ray was emotional as he talked about the immediate aftermath of the storm, and how downed trees and debris kept rescuers from moving his wife out of the rain. They tried CPR on Ruth for about 45 minutes, but her injuries

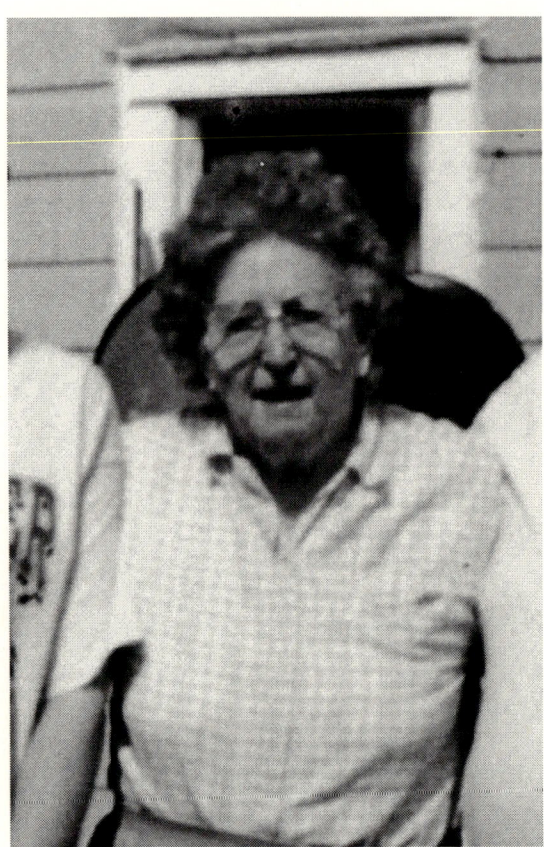

Ruth Schultz, who was in her home in the Town of Dewey with her husband, Ray, and son, Lenny Pfundheller, when the tornado hit. Despite her assurance to her son that she wouldn't die, Ruth succumbed from blunt-force injuries to her chest and abdomen.

were too severe. For Pam, seeing her mother on the ground, rain coming down, lights shining from the ambulance nearby, the house gone, all added to the nightmare that was the reality of this night.

Eighty-year-old Ruth Schultz died outside of the home (in the town of Dewey east of Siren) she had lived in for the past 40 years. Killed from blunt injuries to her chest and ab-domen, after she was hit by flying debris and pushed into a countertop. Ruth's husband, Ray, also suffered injuries. His leg was badly bruised, and he had to have stitches on his head. Sand ended up between his toes, even though he had shoes and socks on. It had to be scrubbed out of his hair.

Ruth Schultz was born in Shell Lake in a birthing house. She lived in the area all her life, except for a few years during World War II, when she worked in an airplane factory in the west. Ray Schultz was a bachelor before he married Ruth, a widow with four children, 28 years ago. Like Ruth, he was a Shell Lake native, and had worked at Penta Wood Products in Siren until the plant closed a few years ago. Ruth worked at one time as a nursing assistant at the hospital and nursing home in Spooner, east of Siren. She also worked for the Stokely/Seneca Company.

Pam, the youngest of Ruth's children, was Ray's shadow, as she had been a shadow to her father, who died when Pam was 11 years old. Ray let Pam drive his car when she was learning to drive. Pam said her mother liked to garden. While the amount of gardening she did herself dwindled during the last few years, the first thing she would do when visiting Pam and Randy was run to Pam's garden to see what was growing.

"(Ruth) was a very nice lady. I've known her for years," her friend, Bev Boyd, said. "She liked to fish—she and Ray together. Wherever they went, they were together; she and Ray, always together."

Ray Schultz, the husband of Ruth Schultz, who died from injuries suffered in the tornado, looked at what was left of his Town of Dewey home after returning from the hospital. With Schultz is a granddaughter from Racine. Photo courtesy of Inter-County Leader.

Sylvan Stellrecht was alone at his home near Poquette Lake when the tornado hit. His body was found after a long search by his children, Julie Melton and Ron Stellrecht, in the woods below his house.

A Family's Loss

"He was a decent, hard-working, honest man who always paid his bills."

—*Shirley Stellrecht, victim's wife*

By Nancy Jappe

Sylvan Stellrecht was the third person killed as a result of the horrific tornado. The 77 year old was alone at the time, and was found dead in the yard of his home on Spaulding Road in the Town of Dewey east of Siren. According to Burnett County Medical Examiner Pat Taylor, he died of trauma, head and neck injuries.

A deeply personal man, Stellrecht's family chose to honor him by keeping the details of his life private following his death, believing that is what he would have wanted.

The following is the only comment his wife, Shirley Stellrecht, wanted included in this book: "He was a decent, hard-working, honest man who always paid his bills."

Searching for Survivors

"Thus it is of the utmost importance in all emergencies to control one's inner self for the present crisis. Place a hand of steel upon brain and nerves, and calmly and prayerfully, await results. They are, as a rule, in one's favor."

—*Mary Adeline Boehm, June 12, 1899*
The New Richmond Cyclone

Firefighters checked homes throughout the village of Siren in the hours after the tornado touchdown. Right next to this house, a smaller house was untouched; and a couple, in their 90s, chose to ride out the storm and remain in their home, despite offers to take them to a shelter. Photo courtesy of Inter-County Leader.

Sounding A Warning

"God, don't let me die. I want to go to my daughter's wedding."

—*Dean Roland, Siren Police Chief*

By Nancy Jappe

Siren Police Chief Dean Roland was at home paying bills when he first learned the weather conditions in the Siren area were rapidly taking a turn for the worse. It was about 7:35 in the evening, and he was hearing television reports of possible tornado activity and an actual tornado sighting west of Pine City traveling east—right toward Siren.

"I knew Siren didn't have any officers on duty. I told my wife, Shelly, got dressed and went to work. I was out on the street by 7:45 P.M.," Roland said. "While I was driving around, watching things, I heard the local radio station, 104.9 out of Shell Lake, stop all broadcasting to report on the weather. I was also talking to Burnett County Deputy Ron Wilhelm in Grantsburg and Deputy George Felix in Webster."

At 8:05, Chief Roland started telling people to hit the basement and take cover. He tried to find anyone he could and started driving faster, the squad car's overhead lights and public-address system on. People were standing outside Main Street Market, the Holiday Station and the theater. Theater staff asked Roland to swing by if he had anything definite to report.

Roland used his cell phone to call the motels. He called Shelly to tell her to get ready, stopped at the Pine Wood Motel to alert the manager, and went down by the Siren Courts Mobile Home Park. "I'm going to stand and watch it," was the reaction of one trailer park resident.

Roland made so many stops in those few critical minutes before the tornado, he doesn't remember all the places he went to alert people. Later, people would tell him that he had been to this place and that, shouting at people to take cover. He does remember checking to see if the summer hosts at Crooked Lake Park were in their trailer (they were not), and telling theater staff, "Get ready. Here it comes." He was simply working on automatic pilot, moving as quickly as he could. Roland also knew that the town's warning siren had been damaged during a spring storm, and was not functioning. "This was also the reason I was out working to warn people," he said.

By this time, Deputy Wilhelm had reported the tornado would be in Siren in a few minutes. Deputy Felix filled him in on all the rain

Siren Police Chief Dean Roland accepts from Frank Ball (R), of the Minnesota Department of Public Safety, a Minnesota Public Safety Service award for his actions the night of the tornado. Due to his efforts, Roland was able to warn dozens of residents of the impending disaster, possibly saving many lives. The man on the left in the picture is Craig Anderson of the Minnetrista Public Safety Department. Chief Roland went to the Northland Inn, Brooklyn Center, Minn., to receive the award. Photo courtesy of Inter-County Leader.

and hail in the Webster area, directly north of Siren.

When he couldn't find any more people in the village to tell, Chief Roland went along Highway 70 to Nyberg Road on the west side of the village limits, looking for the storm. He was standing beside the squad car when Village Board member Lee Shafer went by, asking Roland what was going on. The police chief told him of the approaching storm, and Shafer headed for home. (He just made it into his garage, when the tornado struck his property.

He was not injured, but had roof and property damage.)

Chief Roland was by the Siren Fire Hall when he got hit by a puff of air from his left. He looked up and saw the air was swirling slowly, so slowly. The cloud ceiling was just 300–400 feet above him. He told the dispatcher that he couldn't see a funnel; the sky was like a fog bank slowly approaching. Then he saw that the clouds were going in different directions. "That is weird. That is a tornado," he said to himself as he saw debris come toward him. He took off, intent on getting home and into his basement. He quickly realized this was futile; he wasn't going to make it home, even though he was just one block away.

He pulled under the overhang in front of a truck and tractor business. By this time, he estimated that the winds were going 100 miles an hour. He watched branches snap off, and a 30-foot flagpole twist 360 degrees and break off at the ground. He saw the roof of the Covenant Church across the highway moving in and out. "Pulsating," he called it. Everything that went flying by sparkled inside because of all the debris that had been picked up.

The sound was like being in the middle of a jet-engine roar. Dumpsters from Creative Jewelers a block to the south went flying by. Then the squad car started bucking and moving forward. "This is the dumbest thing I have ever done," Chief Roland said to himself. "God, don't let me die. I want to go to my daughter's wedding (scheduled for Saturday, July 21, in Idaho)." Afraid the car's roof would cave in, Roland tried to get out, but quickly had to get back in again. He could see the wind go first one direction, then the other.

When he was finally able to make his way home, the fencing was bent and trees were down all around. He went running to the door to meet Shelly. She was not hurt. They said they loved each other, and Roland was off again.

As he made his way toward the north end of town, the sight is one he will never forget. Near Siren's drug store, the street was littered with cars, and he could see that buildings were gone. People came out to meet him. He got on the radio to ask for ambulances, paramedics and emergency people. "Siren is gone," he said.

He got to Auto Stop, a convenience store, only to find that the building wasn't there. He got out of the car, yelling for people to get out of their bathroom shelter. Everyone was safe. He checked the dental clinic, the chiropractic office and the drug store. Roland and Kathy Howe, an off-duty Burnett County Sheriff's dispatcher, put together a command post before Kathy's husband, Siren Fire Chief Tom Howe, got there. Then Chief Roland started looking for people.

"When I saw Auto Stop, I knew we were in trouble," he said later. "I really expected 200-300 people to be injured and 20-30 dead when I called for help. I couldn't believe we were not finding people dead. For four or five hours, I kept wondering how many bodies we were going to find. We didn't find any injured or dead. I was in shock for quite awhile and cried for about eight days. About the ninth day, I stopped crying."

In the days after the tornado, many would credit Roland's heroics as a primary reason no one died that horrible night in the village of Siren.

Putting Aside Personal Loss

"I have been involved with shootings, all kinds of death and fires. I never could have imagined this."

—Wade Wambolt, Siren Volunteer Firefighter

By Nancy Jappe

Firefighters Wade Wambolt and Chris Sybers stood in the middle of Hanson Street, outside the Siren Fire Hall, watching as the tornado barreled its way east toward Siren. "You know the curiosity of firemen," Wade commented later. They could feel the wind come up behind and see the wind pick up debris as it sped toward them.

"Look, a funnel is on the ground," Chris hollered. He and Wade headed back to the fire hall, running to get out of the way of the flying debris, and tried, unsuccessfully, to slam the main door down. The fire hall was an old creamery, a concrete structure. As they stood there, others were inside the bathroom, the safest spot in a tornado.

Chris, who was already in his firefighter gear, stood by the door. He watched trees and boards go by, giving the men inside a play-by-play description of what was happening. A lot of rain was coming down. As they finally got the door shut, debris began slamming against the building.

Wade got his gear on. "I figured we were going to be working," he said. Without elec-tricity, it was difficult to get the main doors of the fire hall open. However, Wade and Chris were able to get the department's rescue truck out and took off first to the home of Wade's in-laws. The whole family was there, including Wade's wife, Kim, and their two daughters. They had been out of town camping and had just returned to Siren. Everyone there was un-harmed. The only damage: a broken window in Wade's Tahoe.

After finding out everyone there was fine, Wade and Chris headed toward the center of town. They went through the south intersec-tion of Highways 35 and 70, and as they drove past the bank a couple of blocks farther north, they got their first glimpse of the tornado's de-structive path. They looked over at each other. "I was in awe," Wade said. "You couldn't plan for this. I have been involved with shootings, all kinds of death and fires. I never could have imagined this."

They first stopped the truck by the Pour House, a restaurant and bar right on the main highway through town. There was a report that somebody was trapped behind the restaurant.

Wade's parents lived there, in a house on Third Avenue, a block east of Wade's own home. He and Chris had an unspoken understanding that this was where Wade would go first. He dropped Chris off and continued on.

"I got to the Auto Stop and saw the destruction. I had just a very empty feeling that is hard to describe because (everything) was such a mess," Wambolt said. "I saw the bareness by my house and couldn't see my mom and dad's house at that time. I took off at full sprint down the road. This wasn't easy, with power lines and fencing down, and debris all over."

He ended up crawling over trees and parts of buildings that were in the front yard of his parents' house. The first thing he could see was his mother, standing in the midst of the rubble, holding her puppy. The walls were out, windows gone, doors were blown off; but his parents, who were in the basement when the tornado hit, were not even bruised. They each got a big hug from their son.

"I am OK. I can stay here," Arnold Wambolt kept saying.

"No, Dad, gas is leaking and a lot of things are happening," Wade replied. "You don't understand what the town looks like." It took the next 45 minutes to get the elder Wambolts from the house to the fire truck.

Eventually, Wade got them safely to Wade's in-laws. He gave his wife Kim instructions to take his parents and the children to someplace safe with electricity, and to call and let him know where they were. By 10 P.M., they made it to Luck south of Siren and got a room at a motel there.

In the meantime, Wambolt went back to help the search-and-rescue team. He and others went house to house on Third and Fourth Avenues, working with the fire departments from Luck, Grantsburg and Webster. The Luck Fire Department was involved in the storm cleanup in Balsam Lake just a few weeks before. "That was a good feeling to see that they knew what they were doing," Wambolt said, "and that everybody was working together."

When he had left for a firefighter training exercise that day, Wambolt had carefully shut every window, every bedroom door, pulled the drapes and shut off the air-conditioning. When he was able to get back to the house in the early-morning hours, with firefighter Kent Lindquist and two flashlights, he found that the doors were broken off their hinges. The basement door was also open, and all the snowmobile gear and winter clothing stored down there were gone.

When he got to the bedroom area, he saw his godson, Weston Anton's, picture looking at him, glass unbroken. The picture had been in a room on the opposite side of the house. "I picked it up and took it with me," Wambolt said, "along with some personal belongings to avoid looters."

The Wambolts lost all their furniture and appliances. Wade lost 95 percent of his clothing; Kim and their daughters about 40 percent because they had clothing with them for camping. But all the angels in daughter Jena's angel collection were in the same spot they had always been. The clock Wade had given Kim on their fifth anniversary was packed with insulation. Wade was able to clean it up, however, and discovered it still worked. Wade's youngest daughter Stephanie's Tupperware toys, stored in boxes, were all over the place. Wade's fishing gear was gone. Some of their wedding pictures were found on Lind Road, a half mile away. They had been upstairs in a closet in the attic.

Debris from the Auto Stop, a convenience store a block west, was inside what had been the Wambolts' home. Rafters, cigarettes, pop, the ballast from light fixtures, all kinds of things ended up there. Four-inch straws were stuck in the oak doors in Jena's room.

The Wambolts had owned the house for seven years. It was an old farmhouse that had been moved to town. The Wambolts had completely remodeled it. Now it was all gone.

After they left his home, Wade and fellow firefighter, Kent Lindquist, went to the elder Wambolts' house to get their prescription medications and to collect a few belongings; they hid them in the fire station that night, just to be sure looters couldn't take them. Then they went to the command post and talked with people there. Later, they went around the village a second time to see if anyone was trapped or injured.

At sunrise, the full extent of the destruction was apparent. "It was an eerie feeling. Everything was gone," Wambolt said. Even the water tower on the south side of the village, which had been hidden by trees, was now visible from the north end.

By 6:30 or 7 A.M., Wambolt asked to be relieved from his firefighter duties to go home to pick up belongings, handle insurance, etc. He spent the first three hours by himself, wandering around and talking with neighbors who were still there, before Kim and the rest of the family came back to town. Volunteers started showing up. One became a permanent member of the Wambolt family. Wade now calls her their guardian angel.

Peggy Simonsen is a schoolteacher from Red Wing, Minn., who has a cabin on Clam Lake. She came in as a volunteer, and took over as coordinator of the cleanup effort at the Wambolts', speaking for the family when they were not there, directing other volunteers on what to do. By Wednesday, two days after the tornado, the two Wambolt homes were cleared and picked up.

Additional stress came Tuesday night, the day after the tornado. Wade's pager went off to respond to an automobile accident. His wife Kim was the driver of one of the vehicles. He drove her to the emergency room at St. Croix hospital, and waited while her injuries were treated. Thankfully, she only had minor injuries.

A day and a half after the storm, Wade suddenly realized he had only had one bottle of water to drink during that entire time. And hadn't had anything to eat

During the most difficult times since the storm, Wade has talked with fire chief Tom Howe and firefighter Chris Sybers. "I learned to deal with it," Wade says. "You have to move on. You can replace a house with a new house. There were no deaths in the family, or friends deceased." And Wade has found comfort in the generosity of others. Old friends and relatives he hasn't seen in a long time have sent stuff or money. An uncle from California even drove all the way to Siren just to see if they were okay.

After all others did to help his family, Wambolt hopes someday to repay the kindness. "I know what is going to happen if (a disaster of this type) happens somewhere else," Wambolt said. "I will drop whatever I am doing to go somewhere else."

On August 7th, an anxious Wambolt family

moved into a new manufactured home on the site where the old house had stood. The new house is totally different from the old. For one thing, it has two bathrooms, where there was only one before. "Wade will love this, living with three women," Kim said, a smile lighting her face. Another plus for the new house, everything in the home is on one level. The best thing, however, is having a home of their own again, after seven weeks without one.

First Response

"You shut everything out and do your job. You don't think of anything until later."

—Chris Sybers, Siren Volunteer Firefighter

By Nancy Jappe

Since Siren's warning system was hit by lightning and severely damaged in April, firefighter Chris Sybers had been working to get a new one. The broken siren was so old, that replacement parts were not available. Sybers and others had set up an appointment with someone from the Federal Emergency Management Agency to discuss available funding for a new siren. It was scheduled for Thursday, June 21. As it would turn out, three days after the devastating tornado struck the town.

"The next you know, this is what happens," Sybers said, with regret in his voice over the coincidence.

Sybers was at the Siren Fire Hall the night of the tornado for a training exercise. After the session wrapped up, the guys who were there were waiting for some of their other friends to arrive from another meeting. They were thinking of going to Siren's new Dairy Queen when their pagers went off.

Sybers called his wife Stacy to tell her to go to the basement and take the scanner with her. And he told Stacy to call her mother, Joyce Kemp, and tell her to go downstairs as well. "I am not coming home, I will do more good here. I will be fine," Sybers told his wife.

"You shut everything out and do your job," Sybers explained later. "You don't think of anything until later. You have a job to do and you just do it to the best of your ability at the time."

He got dressed in his firefighter gear and went outside to check the skies. Siren Police Chief Dean Roland swung around and said, "It's coming." "Yah, we can see," Sybers answered. He watched as the big black wall rolled into town and debris flew around with it.

More than a month after the tornado, Sybers can still recall in vivid detail the scene that greeted him and fellow Siren firefighter Wade Wambolt as they drove the fire/rescue truck into town for the first time. "I saw cars upside down on their tops, listened to people screaming at the Pour House and saw people running all over. It was unreal," he says. "We were going around, doing our job, with an awestruck feeling that, 'there isn't anything here. Where did everything go? Where did everybody go?' We had the realization that there could be many people killed and questioned, 'what are the victims going to do?'"

Sybers thought about the people who might be trapped inside the rubble. He took his orange first-responder bag, equipped with oxygen and other emergency supplies, and headed toward the destroyed houses. He helped to pull people out of their houses, but never had to use the orange bag.

Capeside Cove Good Samaritan Center, a nursing home in Siren, was the first place he checked after the tornado had passed. The residents there were safe. After that, DNR ranger Phil Stromberg and Sybers drove down South Shore Drive, on the north end of town, with other fire personnel. They used a front-end loader to push trees and debris out of the way. They went down Alden Road to check out a report that people there were trapped.

"Nobody was trapped. All along the way, I was checking houses," Sybers said.

Sybers went with members of the Danbury, Webb Lake and Luck fire departments down Lind Road to open up the street. Once there, they fanned out and checked all the houses. Because of all the tornado damage it took them 20 minutes to go less than a mile down Lind Road.

Sybers went back to the command post after that to get water, then went to Mud Hen Lake, west of Siren. Everything checked out there. He finally got back to the command post about 4:30 or 5 A.M. He told the guys that he was going home to get some sleep; he had been up since 5 A.M. the previous day. He went home and took a shower, but couldn't go to bed. He went right back into town, working until 8 P.M.

Sybers figured out later the reason there were no fires from this tornado is because the power had gone out 15 minutes before the storm hit, and gas is lighter than air, meaning it goes up into the atmosphere and dissipates. And under a state mandate, gas tanks at filling stations must have automatic firebreak valves. If a pump falls, the valve shuts off. That may have been a lifesaver at Auto Stop, a gas station on the north end of town completely destroyed by the twister.

After the tornado, Sybers became the right-hand man for Burnett County Emergency Management Director Bobbi Sichta. He worked three weeks with her, attending every meeting of state and federal people, learning the ins and outs of the whole system.

By the end of September, a new, donated siren had been mounted on the existing pole in the center of town, and was waiting for electrical hookup. The new siren will be a tornado siren, not just a fire siren. (A tornado siren has a different blast and duration.)

"I think it should give everyone a good sense of security," Sybers said. "This was a lesson I hope we will never have to (learn) again."

Trained to Command

"We were overrun with people who wanted to help. We had people everywhere."

—Tom Howe, Siren Fire Chief

By Nancy Jappe

Siren Fire Chief Tom Howe has dedicated much of his life to helping others. He's been a member of the fire department for 18 years, the ambulance service for 16 years and the Siren Area Lions Club for 19 years.

During his many years on the fire department, he had gone through a lot of training and classes. Preparation that would serve him well as he headed up search and rescue efforts immediately after the twister moved through town.

The night of the tornado he had, in fact, been participating in one of those many training exercises at the Siren Fire Hall. The others were talking about going to the new Dairy Queen later on, but Tom decided to go home just before 8 P.M. When he got inside the house, he heard the Burnett County Sheriff's Department dispatcher say over the scanner a tornado had been spotted near Pine City, Minnesota, west of Siren.

Howe's wife, Kathy, a dispatcher herself, finished her shift at 8 P.M. and also came home. The Howes have no basement under their portion of the double house, they share with Tom's parents, Herb and Helen Howe. But there is a half basement under Tom's parents' side. Howe got his parents, wife, Kathy, and son, Dan, into the basement there. "This doesn't look good," he said. "I'm going to the fire hall to see if there is any way I can blow the siren."

All the relays and breakers in the town's siren had been blown out in an April storm, but with a tornado approaching Tom hoped there was some way to alert residents. Then he stopped short, realizing that the power had gone out and that activating the damaged siren was impossible.

Four firefighters were at the station when the tornado hit: Tom Howe, Chris Sybers, Wade Wambolt and Gene Lund. All of them knew where their families were, and they had all decided their place was to stay at the station. By the time Howe got back there, it was pouring rain and blowing really hard. He parked up next to the entrance and went inside. It wasn't long before the big garage doors started to vibrate and rattle. Through the one window, the men could see trees and debris blowing by. They went into the kitchen, away from the windows.

Several others joined them at the old concrete-block creamery turned fire hall: A couple from the trailer park, and a man, wife and baby who were driving past. At the fire hall, they heard Siren Fire Chief Dean Roland say that he could see the tornado and stuff flying, and that he was going to take cover. Then a short message came over the scanner from Roland: "Send fire trucks, ambulances, everybody you can. Siren is gone."

They opened the doors to the fire station and got a couple of trucks out. Tom went to the corner of Highway 35 and Main Street, doing traffic control until relief came along. Then he got some guys and went down by the Pour House, a restaurant and bar on the north end of town. The highway was blocked with downed power lines and stuff scattered everywhere.

After about 10 minutes, Howe decided to set up a command post by Main Street Market. From that time on, he stayed there and ran the rescue operation until Tuesday evening, going home for only an hour's sleep about 6 A.M. Other rescue workers, who had been up all night, were sent home about this time for rest and showers.

In the first hours after the tornado, Howe helped organize a search of every house and business in Siren. The village was divided up into four sections, with groups of volunteers going from one building to another in each of those sections.

"It was unbelievable that we didn't find someone (trapped), the way the houses and destruction were," Howe said. The searchers found a couple of people with fairly minor injuries. They found people with nowhere to go. But there were no deaths or serious injuries anywhere in the entire village.

Immediately following the tornado, people were sent to the United Methodist Church on First Avenue for shelter, but it quickly became apparent a bigger location was needed. With permission from Jim Bucher, Siren Schools superintendent, two teachers opened the school to be used as a shelter.

As the daylight hours faded away, volunteers worked by the dimming sunlight flooding in from the west-side windows of the school's common's area to set up portable lights. Others equipped the gymnasium with cots for sleeping. The area near the main doorway was used as a sign-in spot—a place to keep track of who came and went.

Siren's fire chief was in the thick of the efforts, using his professional training to organize rescue efforts. "There was so much automatic stuff going on, 'set this up,' 'do this,'" he said. "You were worrying about finding all these people and about volunteers and emergency workers coming in and wanting to do something. You were trying to get them assigned duties that made sense and deciding to do it in a logical manner." There was no time for personal reflection on what had happened. That would not come until later the next day.

Within an hour of the tornado, emergency personnel from towns around northwestern Wisconsin were flooding onto the scene. "We were overrun with people who wanted to help," Howe said. "We had people everywhere." The challenge in having all this help was to be systematic in what was being done. When they were out on search and rescue missions, workers were told to go only where they were assigned. Once that search was completed, they had to return to the command post for another assignment.

Early the next morning, crews had fanned out across the county for an exhaustive building-by-building search of the tornado's entire path. While a second search of the village proper was going on, rescuers headed out toward Mud Hen Lake, three miles directly west of Siren, and continued their search as far as Range Line Road, where the tornado had started. In the eastern part of the county, personnel from the St. Croix Hertel Fire Department looked for survivors. Howe was listening to them on the radio and sending help where it was needed.

"We didn't miss anything," Howe said. "We found people who were still in their houses but were okay. They just couldn't get out of their driveways. Some people were happy to be where they were. We documented where they were, and asked if they need assistance. By 4 A.M. Tuesday, we were 99 percent sure we had searched every building in the path of the tornado."

One of the main concerns was the possibility of fires or explosions from gas leaks in buildings or residences. Wisconsin Gas Company shut off the lines feeding gas to the entire area, while residents like Joel Struck and Wade Wambolt went out themselves to turn gas off, hearing the sound of hissing as the gas escaped from broken lines. Electric power had gone off before the tornado hit.

During one of his breaks from the command post, Howe was near where the Auto Stop convenience store had been destroyed on the north end of town, when he saw a worker about to light up a cigarette. "Put that cigarette out!" Howe shouted at him.

A burning ban in the village lasted until Monday, July 23. "The town would have been a dense cloud for a week (without the ban)," Howe commented.

During the hours immediately after the tornado, the fire chief says he was able to focus on his job because he knew his own family was okay. Howe's son, Danny, had reassured him that, although his brother John's house on Herman Johnson Road had been destroyed, John and his family were safe. Howe already knew that his other brother Jeff's business, The Shops at the Lodge, was gone, but that Jeff and his family were safe as well.

"I have got to believe that for some reason or other, God was working, and that God wanted me to do my thing," Howe said. "I didn't have branches blown off my trees or trees down (in my yard). My family was secure, and I could leave them here and go to the fire station thinking, 'I have got to go and do this because the town is going to need help.' I didn't have to worry about my own family. This took my focus off them."

Like many others in Siren after the tornado, Howe was impressed by the massive outpouring of support. "For not really ever having a major disaster in the county, I was surprised by how fast the emergency government got its act together and showed up with a trailer, and how fast the Red Cross and Salvation Army hit town," Howe said. "If there is a tornado somewhere near by, I will be one of the first persons getting people to help out. It is unbelievable the way people helped us. I think everybody did a hell of a job, as far as I am concerned."

Experience is the Best Teacher

"We learned more from this experience than we ever would have during an exercise."

—*Bobbi Sichta, Burnett County Emergency Management Director*

By Nancy Jappe

Burnett County Emergency Management Director Bobbi Sichta is a trained weather spotter and ham radio operator who lives in the countryside about 10 miles north of Spooner, Wisconsin.

On the night of Monday, June 18, she was glued to her weather-monitoring equipment, tracing a storm that started out in Pine County, Minnesota, before 8 P.M. When she heard funnels were coming from the clouds in the unincorporated communities of Falun and Alpha, she headed for Siren, stopping twice along the way because of the heavy rain and hail. Sichta didn't dwell on what was happening; there was no time for that. She was too busy calling personnel on her car phone, coordinating emergency response efforts.

The Wisconsin State Patrol had already put up barricades at the north junction of Highways 35 and 70 by the time Sichta got to Siren about 9 P.M. She went through the barricades and headed into the village, looking for Burnett County Chief Deputy Don Taylor and Siren Police Chief Tom Howe.

The two were already in the parking lot by Main Street Market in the center of town, having decided this was the best location for a command post. The North Ambulance Service command vehicle from the Webster Fire Station was on the scene. (The vehicle contains radios for use by amateur radio personnel and volunteer dispatchers.) Sichta surveyed the scene a little differently than others. When she saw all the destruction, churning through her mind were thoughts of how to respond.

The parking lot, by this time, was covered by a mass of people, moving in every direction, working to get organized. Sichta immediately recognized Chief Deputy Don Taylor's natural abilities to take charge in a chaotic situation. "He was completely calm and in control, the right kind of guy to have in an emergency," she said. "He is one who knows what he is doing and doesn't get riled." The first priority for the emergency workers was search and rescue, sending teams out to make sure they systematically covered every corner of the tornado's path.

Right away Sichta knew they would have to open a shelter at the school and get it staffed. They also needed an emergency operations center (EOC) at the Burnett County Government Center to handle telephone calls and volunteer efforts. The EOC was important because it had a bank of phones they could use to coordinate emergency efforts. Sichta's staff kept track of the calls they were getting starting at 11 P.M. the night of the tornado, with numerous volunteers helping staff the EOC and answer the phones.

Besides getting the shelter opened, Sichta had to make sure cots and blankets, stored at the Burnett County Airport, got to the school. On her way to Siren, she had stopped in Spooner to pick up coffee and sandwiches to hand out before other emergency response teams arrived. Soon after midnight, the Salvation Army came into town with large quantities of food for the victims.

Even though there was damage to his building, Main Street Market Manager Scott Hickethier opened the doors of his store to the emergency personnel, telling them to take whatever they needed and continually asking if there was anything he could get them.

Bobbi Sichta, Burnett County's emergency management director, received a bouquet of yellow roses from the county board of supervisors in appreciation for her efforts following the tornado. At the meeting, the county board passed a resolution commending county employees for their exceptional performance and dedication following the tornado. "I don't think there was a department in this building that didn't send people down," Sichta said. Photo courtesy of Inter-County Leader.

By 6 A.M. Tuesday, June 19, the Salvation Army had its food wagon going. Last year, county personnel and volunteers had taken training on how to set up a Red Cross shelter. This was their first experience putting that training into action.

The day after the tornado, Sichta was overwhelmed by the number of volunteers showing up to help. By that afternoon she knew that, with the other responsibilities her small staff had to handle, managing all those volunteers would be too much. To help, she called on Ed Forrester and others from the Wisconsin Department of Natural Resources. She knew they were trained to coordinate volunteers to fight forest fires. During the next 10 days, more than 60 DNR staff members were on hand to lend their support managing the volunteer efforts. "They were lifesavers," Sichta said, adding that this was the first time the DNR has been used in Wisconsin to assist a county after a natural disaster. "I can't say enough about the DNR help. People need to know what an asset they were."

From the start of the tornado-rescue effort until Friday, July 27, nearly six weeks later, Sichta's office logged 15,000 volunteers into their records. She is sure that probably 3,000 to 4,000 more never signed a volunteer sheet.

There were also many others whose efforts were of great help to Sichta's office in the days after the tornado. Among them, volunteers at the Rusk Town Hall. The town board opened the doors there, providing a place to feed people on the eastern side of the tornado's path. Another big help were employees of the St. Croix Tribe, who provided numerous meals. (Where else would volunteers be fed prime rib brought over from the Turtle Lake Casino?)

The ironic part about the tornado is the village of Siren had already been chosen to participate in a two-year, tornado-disaster exercise. Sichta had already had one planning meeting with Siren Police Chief Dean Roland before June 18. The plan was to have several of these meetings with various community groups over a one-year period. During the second year, each individual agency would then test the procedures they had in place to respond to a real tornado. The final exercise would put the skills of all the agencies into action together.

That exercise was wiped out June 18. "We learned more from this experience than we ever would have during any exercise," Sichta said. The emergency crews will go through individual and department-wide debriefings this fall, to share the knowledge they gained with one another.

Reflecting back, Sichta said: "I am very proud of the coordinated response and recovery efforts made by our responders."

❧

Duty Calls

"It went really well. It was amazing how smoothly it went."

—Donald Taylor, Burnett County Chief Deputy

By Nancy Jappe

Donald Taylor is a law enforcement veteran. Taylor has been in the field since 1977, and has served four terms as Burnett County Sheriff. Currently he is second in command of the department in the permanent position of chief deputy. Those years of training and experience would pay off the night of June 18, as Taylor headed into the Siren area to play a critical role in dealing with destruction left in the tornado's path.

He had worked late that night and got home for dinner around 7 P.M. The television was on with a weather warning flickering across the screen. Reports from the National Weather Service and the voice of Burnett County Sheriff's Deputy Ron Wilhelm came through on the police scanner, telling everyone the storm was in Grantsburg, headed east toward Siren. A little while later, the voice of Siren Police Chief Dean Roland came across saying Siren had been hit hard.

Taylor and his wife, Jeanne, got into the car just about the time hail started falling. "We are not going anywhere," he said. "Let's get out of here." The hail varied from the size of marbles to softballs. The two followed the eaves of their house for shelter and got inside their basement door. They watched as the storm quickly passed. Then they got back into the car and headed toward town. On the way in, Taylor contacted Polk County, asking for as many ambulances as they could spare. About 15 of them responded quickly to that request.

Pine trees blocking the highway beside the Syren General Store on the north edge of Siren were Taylor's first indication of damage. Someone nearby had a chainsaw, which they used to cut a hole through the branches to let Taylor into town. After a quick look around, the chief deputy began helping set up a command post outside the grocery store in the center of town. At the time, he wasn't thinking of anything other than the task at hand. "That is standard law enforcement procedure," he said. "You do what you have to do and don't think beyond." (He explained that in some ways it's a self-defense mechanism that helps people who respond to emergency situations cope with what is happening. They block out their own emotions, so they can get their job done.) He initially thought the command post should be on Main Street. Then someone suggested that being right on Hwy. 35/70 by the grocery store would be a better location.

No shelter was available until a trailer provided by Wisconsin Emergency Management Services arrived from Menomonie about 1 or 2 A.M. The fire department command post was set up in the same central location. Rick Risler, assistant director of Wisconsin Emergency Management Services, brought the trailer to Siren. Risler asked what was needed. "I need 30 cops by 8 A.M.," Taylor said. As requested, those officers were there by 8 A.M.

As efforts got underway to establish a command post, officers and firefighters fanned out across the village, going to homes to see if anyone was hurt, lost or dead. "Everyone (from the sheriff's department) who was here came (in)," Taylor said. "When something like that happens, everyone comes."

For the next week, Taylor barely got out of Siren. His hours were double what they normally would have been. He was there right after the tornado hit until about 2:30 P.M. the next day. He then went home for a few hours break, came back at 8:30 P.M. and worked straight through until 8 the next night. At this point, he was mostly dealing with traffic issues.

Taylor handled the command post as far as the sheriff's department was concerned, telling people where they should go and what they should do. "The turnout was incredible, not only in people but equipment," Taylor said.

"The St. Croix Tribe sent all of its construction equipment. They were here to work and went out and cleared roads and checked houses."

The Rusk and Douglas County sheriffs also came to help Taylor at the command post. After they had checked the area for people trapped in their demolished houses, the officers kept busy controlling traffic. When there wasn't a need for their expertise as officers, many volunteered to go out and cut wood.

Reflecting back on what happened, Taylor believes the reason there weren't more injuries or deaths was because of the time of day the tornado hit. People could see the tornado coming, and most everyone took some type of cover. There were also many warnings from a number of sources, including scanners, television and people contacting one another.

If a tornado were ever to strike the Siren area again, Taylor says he wouldn't do anything differently. "It went really well. It was amazing how smoothly it went. A nice thing when you have an emergency situation is that people don't question you. All they want to do is help."

For the first few nights after the tornado, Taylor reacted like the well-trained law enforcement official that he is. But later, his personal feelings about what happened crept in. One night going home, he drove down Herman Johnson Road, along Clam Lake east of Siren. It was then that he allowed himself to realize the extent of the damage. "Holy cow," he thought, as his mind finally had a chance to process the power of the tornado.

Chad Thomas, Duluth, Minn., Channel 3 reporter and Siren native interviewed Burnett County Sheriff Tim Curtin in the days following the tornado. Thomas is the editor of this tornado-memory book. Photo courtesy of Inter-County Leader.

The Challenges

"My role was to offer suggestions and direction, and help coordinate with other agencies. I believe I did a good job."

—*Tim Curtin, Burnett County Sheriff*

By Tim Curtin

We have a wonderful community where people pull together at times like the tornado. I felt my role was more of a supervisory one—that of stepping back and looking at what needed to be done and the direction necessary to go in, rather than being hands on. We had officers and administrative staff whose job it was to be the hands-on people. My role was to offer suggestions and direction, and help coordinate with other agencies. I believe I did a good job.

One of my main roles early on was also to be a liaison with the media. I believe the cooperative effort with all the agencies worked better than having any one agency or person in charge.

Is there room for improvement? We are always looking to improve ourselves and the quality service we give.

I think the town chairmen did a tremendous job. For them to step forward was just a fantastic effort on behalf of the people who elected them.

Picking up the Pieces Together

"It was not long before New Richmond was a busy trading center again. Enterprise cannot be blown away by storm or drowned by flood."

—*Mary Adeline Boehm, June 12, 1899*
The New Richmond Cyclone

Saying Thank You

"They had a Godly attitude."

—Siren Resident Howard Kopecky, talking about the volunteers

By Nancy Daniels

Howard Kopecky is no stranger to cleaning up trees and brush piles. For 32 years he taught agriculture and other science courses at Siren High School. During that time he also ran a successful landscape and tree removal business. After retiring two years ago from teaching, he has continued to operate Kopecky Tree Service, Farm and Rental.

A very involved member of the community, it was natural for Howard to volunteer his expertise after the tornado, donating countless hours of his own time and equipment, which included eight chainsaws, a skid steer, a dump truck and a tractor.

Along the way over the next weeks, the 59-year-old met hundreds of volunteers, teaching them the basics of working a chainsaw and overseeing their work. They were from all walks of life, from all parts of the country. He met people from Ohio, Florida, Missouri, California, Illinois, Iowa, Virginia and Minnesota. There were also two people who made the trip from Ontario, Canada. Although the first few days after the tornado were very hot, humid and windy, he did not hear one complaint about the weather or their assigned jobs.

As well as getting volunteer crews started on a job, he would also offer water to the workers and check their pulses. He noticed one man gingerly approach a brush pile, grab, shake and finally pull loose a branch. Howard asked if he could check his pulse. The man said it should be around 74. Howard asked him, "May I ask you what you do for a living?" The man chuckled and replied, "Well, I'm not a professional brush-puller." It turned out he was a cardiac surgeon from the Mayo Clinic in Rochester, Minnesota. He was just in Siren to do what he could to help, and didn't complain once about the heat or the conditions of the job.

He met many people who were highly paid professionals in the computer business who had been fired or laid off within the last 8 months. Howard met three electrical engineers, who, because of the economy, cut backs or mergers, were all out of work. One of them said it was good that he was terminated because it pushed him to work on completing his doctorate in nuclear engineering, something he'd wanted to do for a long time.

He was trying to get a group of kids set up one day for a job but they just sat there. He didn't know if there was something wrong with them, or if they just didn't understand him. So he asked if any of them understood him. One 15-year-old boy with an accent said he did, explaining that the group spoke French. They were from an international youth exchange program through the YMCA at a camp in Amery, Wisconsin, 50 miles south of Siren. This young man could speak English quite well, but Howard found out it was not the only language he spoke. He also knew Spanish and German, but his favorite language to read and study was Greek. Needless to say, he translated quite well for Howard so the group of young travelers could get on with their work.

He met one man who had been in the Green Berets, and had quite a story to tell about how he became one. This man had felt the call to join the armed forces in his early 20s. During his physical, however, it was discovered that he had a heart arrhythmia. Because of this, he was about to be rejected. But he really wanted to serve his country, so he asked if there was any way he could stay. When they found out he was a water safety instructor, it was enough for him to get a waiver for special services. His boot camp would be modified.

Well, after he went through that "modified" boot camp, he thought he surely wouldn't have made it through a regular one. It had been tough. But when all was said and done, he discovered that instead of being assigned to special services, he had been assigned to Special Forces for four years with the Green Berets. His boot camp had not been modified at all. He went on to serve a tour of duty in Vietnam. He had wanted to serve his country, and got the chance to do so.

Five staff members from a nursing home in Fennimore, Wisconsin, located in the southwest corner of the state, approximately 300 miles away, also came to do their part. The director of nurses turned out to be quite a good dump truck driver since she grew up on a farm. And there were many volunteers from Parker Hannifin in Grantsburg, 15 miles away. Their employer gave them the time off to pitch in.

Then there was the group of inmates from a prison in Gordon, Wisconsin, who came with one unarmed supervisor. Howard says they were fantastic young men, who worked very hard. One large man among the group spoke very eloquently, Howard says, sharing his sympathy for what had happened with the people of Siren. Because of this disaster, he was able to have a taste of freedom while he helped.

Reflecting back on those first days after the tornado, Howard says all the volunteers were good-humored and had what he describes as a "Godly attitude." A tragedy like this, he believes, just brings out the best in good people.

Taking Time to Help

> "I was just touched. I had a crew that I could send up there and make a big difference. I was happy to be able to do it."
>
> —Chris Glancey, Glancey Concrete Owner

By Nancy Jappe

Chris Glancey made a spontaneous decision the day after the tornado, after listening to news reports about the tornado that had hit Burnett County. The owner of Glancey Concrete—a five-employee company based in Vadnais Heights Minnesota, a Twin Cities suburb—was working on a job that day that wasn't all that important. Glancey told his crew that he would pay them for eight hours, then sent four of them, and a dump truck, on their way to Siren. He and another man had to stay behind to keep their current job going.

The four men, Blake Kuncl, Ryan Eckert, Nate Fillmore and Jake Kirchner, had no idea what they were going to do once they got to the tornado area. They ended up spending the day in Siren, loading trees onto the dump truck and taking them to the landfill.

"It was a good thing," Glancey said later. "They came back dead-dog tired, but they were happy. One of the guys is only 16. He had to get permission from his parents to go up." Glancey paid the men for eight hours, but they worked longer than that, donating their own time to the tornado-relief effort.

Neither Glancey nor any of his men had any previous connection with Burnett County. About 20 years ago, Glancey helped with tornado relief in Minneapolis. His foreman, on his own, had gone to Granite Falls, Minnesota, to help in the relief efforts there, after a tornado hit that town in July of last year (2000). The foreman was ready and eager to lend a helping hand in Wisconsin, confirmation for Glancey that this was the right thing to do.

"I was just touched," Glancey said. "I had a crew that I could send up there and make a big difference. I was happy to be able to do it."

One of the crew members, a friendly sort of guy, said hello to a woman he met on the streets of Siren. Little did he know that she was a reporter from the Minneapolis Star Tribune or that a picture of the crew would appear in the paper. One of the men came in to work one morning with a copy of the paper in his hand. "Get out of here," Glancey said in surprise, when the man showed him the picture.

Glancey had gone through Siren maybe a time or two in the past, but for some reason, since the tornado he has been in town twice, on

Chris Glancey, owner of Glancey Concrete Products in Vadnais Heights, Minnesota brought his crew of employees to help residents of Siren clean up. Jake Kirchner, Blake Kuncl, Ryan Eckert and Nate Fillmore take a break for lunch in front of Russ' Old Fashioned Meats. Photo courtesy of Star Tribune.

the way to his parents' cabin in Ojibway. Like many others who showed up to help, Siren now means more to Glancey because of the investment he and his men made in the tornado recovery.

An Abundance of Support

"I could fill this book with all of those who helped in some way."

—*Karen Sargent, Siren Resident*

By Karen Sargent

June 18, 2001 is a day we'll always remember. Not only because of the tornado that did so much damage to our quiet, peaceful little town, but also for the way everyone pulled together to help each other. There's the incredible number of volunteers, not only from the towns close by, but St. Paul, Minneapolis, Milwaukee, Chicago, to name only a few. And some even from states as far away as Arizona and Georgia.

These were beautiful people who either experienced a disaster in their town or just wanted to help in any way they could. Law enforcement, medical personnel and disaster teams came from all around. Owners of heavy equipment, so crucial for removing trees from roads and homes, and electric company repair crews, needed to restore power, worked non-stop. In record time, rescue teams went to *every* house hit by the tornado to make sure all the occupants were safe. The clergy and counselors provided an ear to listen and shoulder to cry on.

And I'll never forget our own Police Chief Dean Roland, who risked his life by driving around town getting people off the streets and into safe areas, using his loud speaker to warn

as many as possible of the impending danger of the tornado that Monday night. Then there's Sgt. Karen Felix, who a few days later drove our children around on her 4-wheeler, cheering up a lot of frightened kids who just didn't understand what had happened, or were unable to talk about the destruction.

I could fill this book with all of those who helped in some way. One of the most important disaster teams was the Salvation Army. They were first to get a shelter going for homeless and needy residents, bringing in food and cots and help wherever needed. And they will be the last to leave, making sure any donations of food, money, etc., will be used in this area. I will be proud to ring their bell at Christmas time. The Red Cross was second on the scene, ready to help the Salvation Army provide for the community.

So many groups put on special events to raise much-needed funds to rebuild our town and other areas hit by the tornado. Youth groups from Minnesota, and areas farther away, are still coming to help clean up. These young people have surely made their churches or organizations proud, but not as proud as we feel. We always hear of youth in trouble with the law, drugs and worse acts, but seldom do we hear about those wonderful kids who so often go unnoticed. I guess it's true, "The squeaky wheel gets the attention!" Thanks to each and every one of you.

When we were serving meals, made by a Spooner church, *they* kept saying: "Thank you! Thank you!" I said, "No, thank *you* for all your help!"

Speaking of thank yous, Dean Roland, if it wasn't for your bravery, quick action and dedication to Siren, I really believe we could have lost many more lives. We love you, Dean. You were there when we needed you most!

Another tireless person was Pastor Steve Ward. A strong supporter of the Salvation Army, he worked almost four straight days without sleep, going from place to place wherever he was needed. His wife, Gail, never knew where he was half the time. The only answer Gail knew for sure was: "He isn't fishing!"

My husband of 32 years, Bill, and I were home working and taking care of our two grandsons, Jordan, 8, and A.J., 2, the night of the tornado. (Bill and Karen Sargent live on the eastern side of the village, right across from the school.) Bill decided to go to the Dairy Queen for treats around 8:25 P.M. I was in the kitchen holding A.J., while Jordan was in the front room playing with his new puppy he got the same day. (By the way, we named her Stormy.)

All of a sudden, I looked out the kitchen window and saw my tall shrub lying flat. I didn't even know we were having storm warnings because I had been reading to the boys and didn't have the TV or radio on. I yelled for Jordan to hurry and get in the basement. He wouldn't go

until he had his dog, so I grabbed the dog, threw him in Jordan's arms and carried all three to the basement. Low and behold, toys and clothes were swirling around the basement, like some magic trick. After putting the boys under the steps, I shut the windows, ending the show.

Not once did I think about Bill and where he was until he came in the door, pale as a ghost. I listened, as he recalled what had happened to him. He had been on his way to the Dairy Queen for treats, but when he turned the corner into town all he saw was black sky. He turned around and drove 65 mph home. He made it into the garage, and then, after he got out of the car, the garage windows exploded. He fell (jumped) to the floor, and watched debris float by through the open garage door. Bill said he really thought his time had come! All I could think was, "Thank God he didn't try to make it in the house out of fear for our safety."

While in the basement, it seemed as if all the air was sucked out of the house, and I heard what sounded like a train. It was then that I realized we probably had a tornado touch down very close to our home. The whole incident seemed to last maybe 4–5 seconds. When we did go outside, we knew for sure a tornado had touched down. Outside all we could see were trees down, along with power lines. So many things were missing. Clotheslines that had been full of clothes were now empty.

I still have a hard time explaining how we felt then because I'm sure both of us were in shock. It was unbelievable that in such a short time, all this damage could happen. Neither of us knew how bad it was up town.

When my daughter Denise (A.J.'s mom) returned home safely, I thanked God for keeping all of my family safe. The radio was reporting that many people were homeless and needed a place to stay, so I went over to the Siren School to help set up a shelter. Also, they wanted everyone to check in to give their names, to figure out who was still missing. I remember how sad it was to see so many bewildered people. A lot of children and babies, even dogs on leashes.

We didn't have any baby bottles so I ran home and got what we had, except for a bottle for A.J. I don't remember how many trips I made home for food, bottles, blankets, stuffed toys, sippy cups to use until I could get to the store in the morning. At 6:00 A.M., still not knowing the condition up town, I walked up there to see if I could find some bottles and peanut butter for the little ones. When I saw how torn up our beautiful town was, I started crying and couldn't stop. Can you imagine a crying 60-year-old woman saying to the owner of Main Street Market, still bawling, "Do you have any baby bottles?" I laugh now when I think of this.

Later in the day I walked down 4th Avenue by myself and was amazed at how many people were clearing areas with their chain saws. There was Lynn (Murphy) Dwire cutting these big tree trunks as easy and swiftly as any man there. I was surprised, but shouldn't have been. That's how Lynn is. She handled that saw like she did it for a living. We hugged, and again I cried all the way home.

We lost four trees in our yard. You couldn't walk around the house because there were so many branches and other debris. But instead of cleaning up the yard, I decided to take a quick nap. I was extremely tired after being at the school all night. A while later when I woke up, probably due to chain saws, a crew was cutting

our trees and was already almost finished. Praise God, I thought, because we didn't even own a saw. (And I didn't want one. Bill would probably cut his leg off!)

It sounds selfish when I think of all those who lost lives and homes, but I really do miss my trees, although my front room is so much lighter. So many mornings we wake up and look outside hoping it was just a bad dream, but it wasn't.

I've always known that Siren people help each other out when times are tough, but, so many strangers worked and sweated to clean up our town in some of the hottest days this summer. When we'd give them water, sandwiches, soda, etc., *they* were so grateful. "Thank you, Thank you," they said. I thought, and told them, they were more than welcome but that we should be thanking them a million times over. These people—*these friends*—are definitely angels from heaven.

I've heard so many people complain because the town's siren didn't work, but I really don't think it would have mattered. How many of us would have thought anything as bad as this tornado was coming? Besides, we had a siren by the name of Dean Roland, bless him.

I'll always remember walking into the school that night and seeing so many shocked looks on everyone's faces. Just sitting and staring ahead. One particular older gentleman, maybe 90 years old, just sat with an army blanket over his head. All I could see was his eyes and nose. I kept going up to him, offering water, food, anything to make him feel a little better. He never answered me the first four times and I was truly worried about him. He finally said, after I told him that if he just talked to me a little he might feel better, "How can I feel better? I lost my wife

2 years ago. Last month I lost my dog, and tonight I lost my house and everything in it. Why the hell couldn't I have gone up with my house?" This was tough to answer, because I can't say I wouldn't have felt the same.

Siren will recover. That's all we know how to do. Siren residents don't give up without a fight. It may take 5-6 years, but I know Siren will be even more beautiful, with new houses, buildings, and, yes, even trees. We'll be right back in our cars, trying to cross Highway 35, watching car after car after car go by with Minnesota license plates. I, for one, will NEVER complain again about all the Minnesota people coming up here. We wouldn't be this far in our cleanup if it weren't for our friends from Minnesota. Thanks to all of you.

Bill and I will definitely grow old here in Siren.

Pitching In

"I will always be amazed at the selfless generosity and dedication these volunteers put to their task of helping the people of the Siren area."

—*Red Anderson, Lifelong Siren Resident*

By Red Anderson

The day after the tornado, I looked at what used to be a nice little hobby farm, a farm that is now scattered across a field and over a hill. Part of the barn is in the woods across the road to the north. The rest of the barn went northeast. The corncrib went east, while the storage shed next to it went with the barn. The garage, still standing where it had always been, was flattened out, as if a big foot had stepped on it. The house, although damaged, was still there; however, the building next to it was gone. All the trees to the north of the two buildings were leveled. We later counted the loss of 106 trees.

Across the road to the north, I found part of a building that I learned later had come from Siren, 1-1/2 miles away. I wondered what kind of forces Mother Nature brought down on us, to cause so much damage in so many different directions at one time. "Where do we start?" was one of the first questions that came to mind. Broken glass, roofing metal, boards, debris of every description was scattered in all directions. Boards had nails sticking up in them, so we had to watch where we were stepping.

My mind was in denial. This always happens to someone else, not to us. We started picking up salvageble items, making little piles here and there. Then I realized that I had no place to store them. At about that time, two fellows I knew explained that half of the roof on the house was gone. If I could get some tar paper and shingles, they would repair it good enough to keep out any future rain and weather. I didn't even know that the roof was bad!

When I got back with the supplies for the roof, a fellow from Hastings, Minnesota, (who has a cabin on Bass Lake, which is in the Siren area) was there with a chain saw, asking where did I want to pile the tree limbs and brush? I had never seen him before. Before I got him started on the trees, two couples showed up, asking where they could help. Before the day was over, 11 people volunteered for the cleanup. I never found out how they happened to be at our house, but they were welcome and appreciated. Thanks to their help that first day, the roof got a quick fix, broken windows were boarded up and a large dent was made in the debris cleanup.

The man from Hastings came back to help

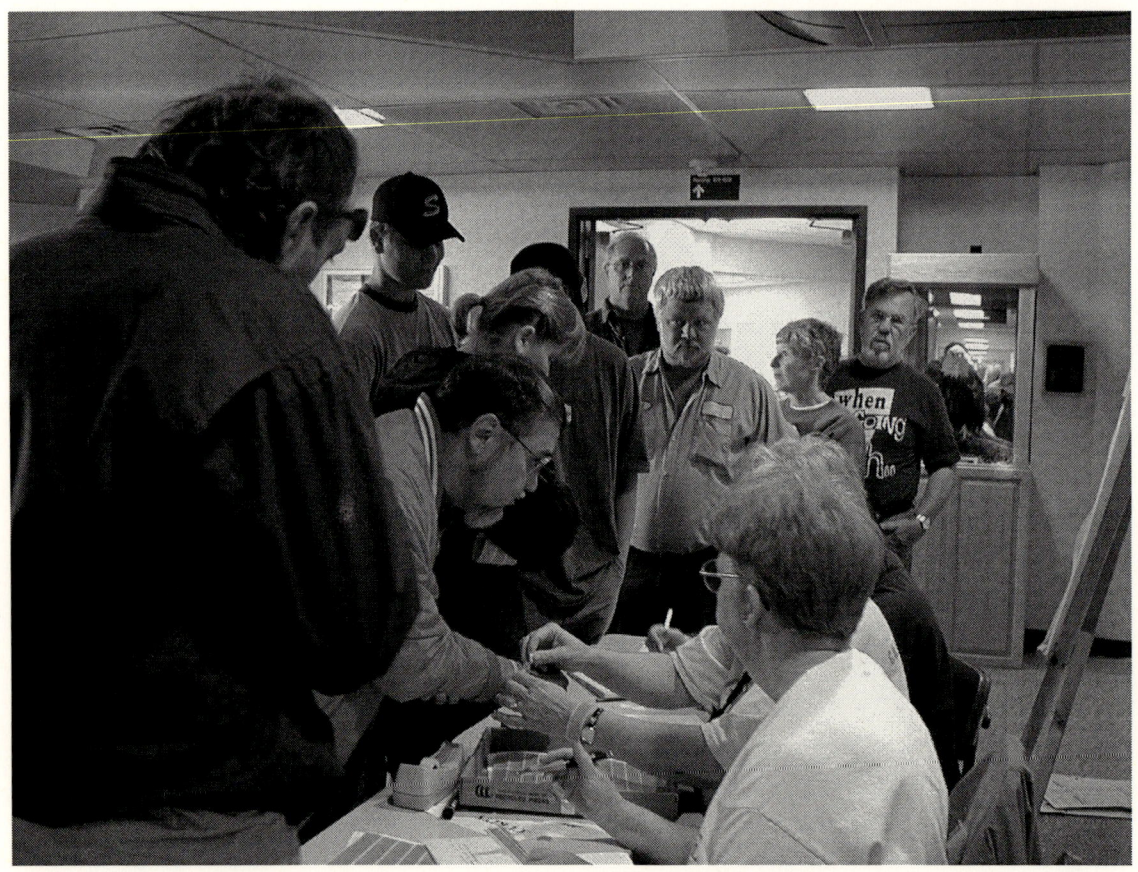

Volunteers lined up at the Burnett County Government Center to get the wristbands that would allow them to enter the village of Siren. Only people wearing the wristband were allowed into the village during the first days of cleanup and recovery. The village was also under a curfew from 8 P.M. to 8 A.M. at first. Photo courtesy of Inter-County Leader.

the second day. About 10 A.M., a Red Cross van came along with food, cold water (very welcome) and treats. They had first aid equipment along with them. They asked if we needed more help. Within an hour, 10–12 members of the St. Croix Tribe, with chain saws, were there to help. They worked with us for the next two days, and were some of the best help a person could want.

On the second or third day, a man, his wife, and 15-year-old son from Minneapolis stopped to help. On their way to Siren from their home, they had purchased a chain saw. One of the Native Americans put the saw together, and gave

them a 10–15-minute lesson on how to run it. At first, I was very concerned about their safety. They turned out to be good learners and very good help.

Our tractor had three flat tires from going over boards with hidden nails. A man from Webster came into the yard with a Caterpillar bulldozer. No flats for that tractor! The dozer was much better for pulling out stumps, pushing trees and pushing debris into piles. The help this man and his equipment brought made everyone's job easier, and guaranteed that the cleanup got done.

For two weeks, volunteers came day after day, working hard. In most cases, they did not know us and will probably never see us again. They came from Minneapolis, St. Paul, Milwaukee, Baraboo, Madison, Prescott, Hastings, Rochester, Balsam Lake, Nebraska and Kansas. Scouts from Boy Scout Troop 127 in Chisago City, Minnesota, came to help, as did our family and friends from Siren, Frederic, Webster and Hertel.

We started each day around 6 A.M. and worked till dark, trying to clean up the mess. It seemed like we had volunteers working right along with us, all the time. During the cleanup, I realized that a change was coming over me. The items in my shop, garage or storage sheds that I had accumulated all my life didn't mean as much to me anymore. My treasures were now just trinkets.

The tornado brought so much damage to everyone in its path. That in itself is some sort of miracle. Towns, and for that matter, the whole country, is growing so fast that some of us have lost touch with our friends and neighbors. Thanks to the tornado, we've had a reminder of what is really important in life, and I believe there was more than one miracle here. Three lives were lost, and that is a tragedy. However, the death and injury rates were so much lower than might have been expected.

Another miracle is the way that the people along the tornado's path have pooled together to show the rest of the country the stuff we are made of. There is not a thing that we could say that would indicate the depth of appreciation and gratitude that is in our hearts for all the spiritual and physical help that so many people have given us. If we are able to do it, it would be a pleasure someday to return these favors.

Red also wrote this short poem about the destruction:

> A silver lining I do not see
> The insurance company seems to have
> the best of me.
> But I will try my darnest to have a clean
> fight
> To assure the future will be bright.

Editor's Note: Siren natives Red and Joyce Anderson have owned a hobby farm on Herman Johnson Road east of Siren for the past 20 years. About a year ago, they moved to a place they own and are remodeling on the Clam River north of Siren. Originally published in the Inter-County Leader newspaper. Reprinted with permission.

The Generosity of Children

"This touched our hearts and brought immediate tears to our eyes."

—*Siren Resident Cathy Hinze, talking about the money her grandsons donated*

By Cathy Hinze, Siren Resident

When the tornado hit Siren, my husband, Norm Hinze, and I were visiting our youngest son and his wife in Australia. We had spent the day on the Great Barrier Reef and when we got back to our hotel I noticed the message light was blinking on the phone.

I mentioned this to Elissa Hinze, our daughter-in-law, and her response was: "Oh, I was supposed to call my parents, but I can do that tomorrow."

After staring at the phone for a few minutes, I said: "No, I left your parents' number with Shane and Rhonda in Siren and I think they are trying to get hold of us." (Shane Hinze is Cathy and Norm's middle son; Rhonda Hinze is his wife.)

Elissa asked: "Do you really think so?" We called her parents and the message was that Shane and Rhonda were ok, but we needed to call Siren right away. When we finally reached Shane at 5:00 A.M., Tuesday, his words were: "Mom, it looks like they dropped a bomb on Siren." He proceeded to tell us all the details.

Before we had left for our trip to Australia, we hired our two grandsons, Jesse, 10, and Elijah, 7, to take care of our dog, Partner. I had distributed the money in envelopes for each one to get $15.00 a week for 3 weeks. They also had to water the flowers and give Partner hugs every day.

When we arrived home June 28th, our family came over to the house and our daughter-in-law, Rhonda, told me this great story about our grandsons. She mentioned to the boys shortly after the storm that they might want to pack up some of their toys to donate to the storm victims, which they did. Then the boys said to their mother: "We also want to donate the money that Grandpa and Grandma Hinze paid us to take care of Partner."

Rhonda took Jesse and Elijah to the Red Cross in Siren. The Red Cross worker looked at Rhonda and said: "What a great mother you must be." As he accepted the money, he turned to my grandsons and said: "Boys, you will be greatly blessed for donating this money."

This touched our hearts and brought immediate tears to our eyes, because Norm and I knew how excited they were to make some cash this summer, and what plans they had made for spending their well-earned money.

A Sense of Community

"A good thing happened for my children, Mike Jr. and Stephanie. They both worked as volunteers and saw firsthand what it means to work together as a community."

—Mike Whiteside, Siren Resident

By Jill Gloodt

Mike Whiteside was home with his son, Mike Jr., when they heard the news of the storm on the television. Mike Sr. went out onto his deck to check the situation. He knew they had to take cover because of the sounds he was hearing.

The sounds of the storm seemed almost familiar to Mike. As a lineman for Polk-Burnett Electric Cooperative, Mike has found himself in several storms, and in the destruction left in their aftermath. He remembers the storm in Canton, a small community near Eau Claire in 1980, where three tornadoes wreaked havoc on the community. And then there were the straight-line winds in Balsam Lake recently that had kept him working 16 hour a days. He knew this wind was different. He knew this was probably going to be bad.

He and his son, Mike, went to the basement immediately. He heard trees cracking, bending and relenting to the powerful wind. They waited for what seemed forever for the sounds of the storm to subside. Eventually they were able to come up from the basement and look around. Both Mike Sr. and Mike Jr. were unprepared for the devastation they witnessed. Mike Sr. said, "I knew I would not be able to get out for a few hours, so I went and got my chainsaw and starting cutting our way out."

While they were cutting trees, Mike Sr. recalls hearing the sounds of emergency sirens. Mike couldn't help but wonder where else the powerful storm had left its mark. Mike Jr. was worried about his sister, Stephanie. Mike Sr. did his best to reassure him that Stephanie would be fine. She worked at the movie theater in Siren; the building was made out of concrete. (At this point, Mike Sr. thought it had only been straight-line winds, and so wasn't as worried about Stephanie as he would have been had he known it was a tornado. Most concrete buildings can easily withstand straight-line winds.)

They both continued cutting trees until they couldn't see any more. Then they both went to bed, sad and exhausted. Many hours later, Stephanie managed to get home through all the debris. "I was so happy to see her," Mike said. Stephanie broke down, telling her dad, "The town is gone."

The morning brought a whole new ball

game. They had to continue cutting their way out of the driveway. Mike Sr. knew that he had some very long days ahead of him. He got to the office not much after daylight. He immediately went into the field to work. He and another crew member, Joe Anderson, spent the day cutting trees, putting lines back up and checking lines to see which buildings could be reconnected with power. He later learned that within a 24-hour period, 45 crew members from the electric company had responded to the call for help.

Mike Sr. explains, "Polk-Burnett uses what is called a Turtle Meter. This is a slow frequency that is sent back through the wires to our substation. We can download from our computer which areas have power and which do not. We can dial up the substation from the field and download all the information we need to get to the people quickly and get their power up and running again. This was what saved us!"

The tornado hit Monday, June 18th. By that Friday, the 22nd, Polk-Burnett Electric was able to send the traveling crews back home. The power was already back on.

After pondering for a minute whether something positive had come from all the destruction, Mike responded, "A good thing happened for my children, Mike Jr. and Stephanie. They both worked as volunteers and saw firsthand what it means to work together as a community."

Endless Hours

> "We're renovating old buildings and constructing new buildings. Although the devastation was profound, Siren is strong!"
>
> —*Rick Anderson, Siren Insurance Agency Owner*

By Jill Gloodt

It had been a busy time for Rick and Jacky Anderson. They'd owned Fishbowl Insurance Agency in Siren since 1988. And in the past few years the area had had two major hailstorms. And then came the tornado . . .

Rick and Jacky had been at a baseball game that night. The umpire had called the game, after seeing lightening. If the ump had not had the good sense to stop the game, Jacky thought later, a busload of children would have been right in the tornado's path.

Once the Andersons got home, they could feel the wind pick up. And then they heard the sound that everyone in a tornado talks about—a freight train. Right after that the phone rang. It was Denise Magnuson, one of their employees. She was crying; her home had nearly been destroyed. Rick and Jacky did their best to console her. They knew they had to get into Siren right away. There would be people who would need their help. They went to their office in the middle of town. It hadn't been damaged. But they could not believe the devastation that was all around.

They immediately opened up their business. The power was out, so Rick and Jacky and one of their employees, Kris Beebee, began working by candlelight. They couldn't fax anything; computers and typewriters would not work. But the phones did. During it all, the phones never went out! They worked through the night consoling people, and calling all the major insurance companies to inform them of the tornado and just how bad it was.

The next morning everyone was frantically working. A family member of Rick and Jacky's (Jill Gloodt, the author of this story) stopped and asked, "What can I do to help?" Without hesitation, they yelled in unison, "Get us some coffee!" Knowing Siren didn't have electricity Jill drove to the bakery in Frederic (10 miles south of Siren) with a very large insulated pot to fill with coffee. The employees at the bakery were filled with questions about the tornado and the devastation. When it came time to pay the bill, the bakery owners wouldn't take any money. After the coffee was delivered, everyone took a few long-awaited sips. But the break didn't last long, there was so much to do.

Angie Gibbs, a former employee, came up

from Madison as soon as she heard the news. She knew she would be able to help. Once Angie arrived, she just rolled up her sleeves and dug in. She would not take any money. Angie stayed three days.

Everyone at the insurance agency was in triage mode. They opened at 6:00 A.M. and didn't close until after 8:00 at night. Most of the catastrophe teams for the various insurance companies were working out of Rick and Jacky's office. Teams that were thankfully trained for situations just like this.

One insurance team member tried several times to get to a client's home, but each time was unable to get through because of the debris. Finally on the fifth or sixth try, she was able to reach a very happy client, who had 32 trees lying on her home.

Rick and Jacky Anderson were tired. When they had a moment to pause and reflect, they thought how hard this had been on them as small business owners. But then Jacky would quickly say, "It's been hard on everyone." Many people had significant losses. In the last three years, the area had gone through two major hailstorms and now an F3 tornado.

Rick and Jacky represent many insurance companies in their business. The Friday before Labor Day weekend, they received a fax from a major insurance company for which they sell policies. The fax said the company would no longer be handling homeowner's or personal automobile insurance. The company held Rick and Jacky's largest line for these two types of insurance. This major company had determined that the monetary losses were too great. "We have no recourse," Rick said. "We are being penalized for something we have no control over." (Editor's Note: Rick and Jacky did not want to specifically name the company in this book.)

In spite of the great losses for many community members, Rick and Jacky see optimism everywhere. "Siren has 21 new buildings going up," Rick said. "We're renovating old buildings and constructing new buildings. Although the devastation was profound, Siren is strong!"

Safe Haven

"Volunteers were serving food to people coming into the commons area. The school would now begin operating 24 hours a day for nearly a month."

—Jim Bucher, Siren Schools Superintendent

By Jim Bucher and Mary Bucher

The evening started with a Building and Grounds Committee meeting in the Siren Schools' District Office. There, along with myself, were school board members, Bill Ellis and Sid Sherstad, and Junior/Senior High School Principal Terry Mengel. At approximately 7:45 P.M., the weather radio came on with an announcement from the Burnett County Sheriff's Department that there was a tornado warning for our area.

At 7:55, my wife Mary telephoned that there was a tornado warning for our area, and that we should head for home. She also called her 87-year-old mother, telling her to take shelter in her bathroom. At 8:05, the weather radio went off again. Due to the approaching storm, we adjourned the meeting five minutes later. Sid Sherstad had walked to the meeting, so I offered him a ride home. We proceeded down South Shore Drive (a road along Crooked Lake, on the north end of Siren) and I let him off in front of his home on Lind Road.

I then turned around and drove back down South Shore Drive to the highway and to our road, North Shore Drive (on the north side of Crooked Lake). I first went into our storage garage across the road from our home to get a portable radio I had there. I drove down our driveway and attempted to open the garage door with the opener. But without electricity, the garage door would not open. I quickly went inside our home through the front door and into the garage and lifted the door by hand. I drove the truck in just as it began to rain and hail. Mary had everything placed under the stairway—a chair, a two-quart bottle of water, flashlight and the cat, Duncan.

The hail now became quite large, the size of a person's fist. We were worried that the hail would break our skylights. The wind was now blowing from the west and the waves on the lake were one and a half feet high with rolling white caps. It was getting darker, and the wind was getting stronger. When we looked out the front windows again, the wind was now blowing from the east, and the waves on the lake were now two feet high. We went back under the stairs.

The radio was still on, with the tornado warning coming loud and clear. It was now 8:25, and the wind had subsided and the sun was shining. We went outside on our deck and looked across the lake and couldn't believe what we saw. The whole south side of Crooked Lake was barren. Trees blown over, metal roofing in the trees, and homes severely damaged. We spoke briefly with our neighbors and then tried to call Mary's mother Alice Mavis. She is physically handicapped, and lived in one of the apartments on 4th Avenue in the village.

Unable to make contact with her, I drove back into town. But due to the downed trees and power lines, I wasn't able to get past Crooked Lake Park. I then turned around and drove to Lind Road, north of town, hoping to be able to drive down South Shore Drive to 4th Avenue and into the apartments. Both roads were blocked at the corner of Lind Road and South Shore. I again turned around and headed for Herman Johnson Road. My plan was to take Herman Johnson Road to County Road B and then down 4th Avenue. No luck. A man and some women were on the road informing everyone of the downed power lines and trees. I turned around and headed home.

Mary and I then took our pontoon boat across Crooked Lake to Beverly and Earnie Swanson's house, hoping we could walk to her mother's apartment. We landed the boat on their beach, and headed to Alice's. As we approached 4th Avenue and saw the destruction, we quickened our pace, climbing over trees and avoiding downed power lines. We could hear chain saws, people calling for help. Then it began to rain. When we finally reached the apartment, it was around 9:30. We were wet and couldn't believe what we saw. Mary became extremely concerned now about her mother's safety. We finally managed to find an opening into the building.

The floor of the apartment had several inches of water on it, and was covered with insulation from the collapsed ceilings. The ceilings and roofs of several of the apartments were completely missing. When we reached Alice's apartment, no one was there. The kitchen, dining area and bathroom ceilings had all collapsed. You could see the sky from inside the bathroom, the place Mary told her to seek shelter. After doing a quick search of the building and finding no one, I headed for the school and Mary went in search of her mother.

By this time, Don Fleischhacker, our Building and Grounds Maintenance Supervisor was in the building along with Chuck Hill, one of the night custodians. Several other staff members started to come in: Darrell Imhoff, an elementary teacher; Ryan Karsten, a junior high teacher; Sheila Staples, our librarian; Jim Hanna, our technology technician; Debbie Jaskolka, our head cook. Each of them immediately began assisting with the disaster relief. The emergency generator was operating, because the power lines were down. Don and Chuck began cleaning up the water damage from the tornado in the junior high wing.

Three of the large roof vents had blown off their housings, puncturing the roof membrane as they rolled across the roof. Two windows in the District Office were broken, along with door glass panes in the elementary wing. Once the building was cleaned up, Don then had to find enough fuel oil to keep the generator running through the night. He and Chuck left with my pickup truck for Yourchuck's, a store one mile north of town, to get diesel fuel.

As the evening wore on, fire-fighting personnel arrived to use the commons area of the school for an emergency response command location. Several local volunteers also began to arrive to lend a hand with the residents who were displaced from their homes. In the large gym, tables were set up to serve food and beverages to the victims, volunteers and emergency personnel. Cots and blankets were also brought in to provide comfort to those who had no place to sleep for the next few nights.

(Editor's Note: Mary Bucher wrote the next part of this story.)

When I left Jim, people wandering on Fourth Avenue directed me to Main Street Market where an emergency center had been established. Emergency vehicle lights lit the street. Right away, I noticed several elderly people being loaded into ambulances. I asked about my mom, but no one knew her whereabouts or condition; however, they offered to check transport logs. Several emergency people asked if they could help; Pastor Jim Carmon from the First Baptist Church of Falun (a tiny community just west of Siren) held my arm and offered to stay with me.

Siren Police Chief Dean Roland (in white shirt on the left), Siren School District Administrator Jim Bucher (with back to camera), Siren School Food Supervisor Deb Jaskolka (in white pants) and volunteers discussed needs during an impromptu meeting at the school, which was used as the Red Cross headquarters throughout the tornado recovery. Photo courtesy of Inter-County Leader.

We kept asking about the elderly people in the Fourth Avenue apartments, when I spotted Mark Foote from Webster. He said that he had seen my mother, and that she was with a family friend of ours, Kathy Howe, a Burnett County Sheriff's Department dispatcher. My mom was all right, he said. Just shook up, but not physically hurt, even though her apartment had collapsed around her. Pastor Jim stayed with me for the next 40 minutes as we searched for Kathy and my mother. Never letting go of my arm, he finally stopped a civil patrol jeep. The driver took me from Kathy's empty house to the Pheasant Inn and then to the Methodist Church. There, an hour after we began our journey, we found Kathy and Siren resident, Howard Kopecky, who told us that they had taken my mother to Capeside Cove Nursing Home.

Our volunteer driver took Kathy and me to Capeside. My mother was there, resting on a padded table in the Physical Therapy Room, where she would spend the night. After a tearful reunion, Kathy and I kissed her good night, and headed for Kathy's house and then the school.

(Editor's Note: Jim Bucher resumes telling the story here.)

I left the school around 11:00 P.M. with Mary and walked back to our pontoon boat. It was extremely dark with no streetlights; the small flashlight we had with us did not provide much light. Crossing the lake by boat with no lights on the shoreline made it difficult to find our way back to our dock. Mary was in the front of the pontoon to look for any floating debris that might be in our path home. After changing into dry clothes and making sure Mary had plenty of candles and a lantern that worked, I drove back to the school around midnight.

By this time the highway was somewhat cleared. Emergency lights were flashing everywhere. When I walked into the gym there were about 150 people spread out. More food had arrived. Siren resident, Donna Tjader, and her sister, Pat Peterson, were in the center of the gym making and handing out sandwiches. People were sitting on the bleachers and folding chairs. At 3 A.M. things were finally quiet in the school, so I headed back home to get some rest.

Mary and I were up at 6 A.M. Tuesday. Our plan was first to check the situation at school to see how things were operating, and then go to Alice's apartment to begin removing her personal items. Two high school boys, Darren Sherstad and Jordan Dailey, and teacher, Ryan Karsten, volunteered to help move things out of the apartment to our garage on North Shore Drive.

Volunteers were serving food to people coming into the commons area. The school would now begin operating 24 hours a day for nearly a month. By now the Red Cross and Salvation Army Disaster teams were also arriving to lend assistance. Various businesses and organizations from as far away as the Twin Cities area began delivering more food, snacks, ice, beverages, bedding, cleaning supplies and clothing. All of which was stored in the large gym, vacant hallways, freezers and coolers. Red Cross and Salvation Army workers distributed the food to workers in town and out in the countryside.

The Red Cross used the library as its center of operations, and the Salvation Army used the small gymnasium. The Federal Emergency Management Agency (FEMA) and Small Business Administration (SBA) set up operations in two high school classrooms and a computer lab. Jim Hanna, the school's technology technician, was stringing wire all over the building for telephone and Internet communications that were needed by these four organizations.

Debbie Jaskolka, our head cook, organized and instructed the volunteers who assisted her in preparing the 98,000+ meals that would be served during this relief effort. As the long days continued, Debbie's voice began to show signs of tiring. She was in the school almost 20 hours a day. One cannot say enough about Debbie, and the time she gave to oversee the kitchen, meal preparation and meal serving. She was the heart of the whole operation.

The custodians were another group of school employees who put their heart and soul into making sure everything in the building was clean and well maintained. They changed their hours so that someone was in the school 24 hours a day to give assistance where and whenever needed.

The tornado damage sustained to the building, playground, track and football field now exceeds $300,000. We never did have a total count of the people who used the school for shelter, meals, showers, etc., but it must have been at least a thousand. I had always hoped and planned for the public to use the school facilities, but I never thought that such a disaster would turn our building into such a valuable community resource.

Lt. Governor Margaret Farrow (L) talks to Deb Jaskolka, Siren School Food Service Supervisor, and Chris Sybers, from the Burnett County emergency management team, during her visit to survey the tornado damage. She spent an afternoon in Siren meeting with local officials. Photo courtesy of Inter-County Leader.

Serving Those in Need

"Together, by early July, we served or delivered nearly 100,000 meals—and that doesn't include the food we gave out the night of the tornado!"

—*Debbie Jaskolka, Siren Schools Head Cook*

By Debbie Jaskolka

The night of the tornado, I walked into the school in Siren to see people already arriving there, some lying on the gym floor. By morning, the gym had turned into a makeshift shelter, with many people spending the night there. Originally we had set up an area in the gym to serve food, but given the large number of people we had to feed we decided to move the food we had to the school's commons area. We also wanted to leave the gym as a place for people to rest, and as a sanctuary for those who were so upset by what had happened.

The power was still out, which made finding things in the school a real challenge. Even the kitchen, which I am very familiar with because I am the school's head cook, was difficult to get around in the dark. Thankfully, someone had brought us a large, portable generator to use—I don't know what we would have done without it. We would fill pots with coffee inside the school, then carry them outside to plug into the generator.

Then, the questions starting coming that had nothing to do with preparing food. The first was, "Debbie, we need to get this lady hooked up to oxygen." I looked. It was Christine Larsen, a woman I have known for a long time. We had to run an extension cord from the generator outside to the inside of the school. Try finding an extension cord in the dark! From there things just started to happen, one after another.

At first, we had just a few Siren School staff members making sandwiches and grilling outside, but before long we had quite an assembly line going. Everyone just pitched in. We had volunteers making deliveries to people out working to clean up the terrible mess. In the beginning, we didn't really know exactly where to send them. We just told them to head out, and offer sandwiches, chips and beverages to anyone they saw.

That first morning, the donations that came pouring in were unbelievable. That's what kept us going. I didn't keep records of this at first. But after meeting with the Red Cross and Salvation Army, they told me I needed to do this. I didn't think it would be a problem, but people were giving so much, that I know I missed some items. It started to hit me then, what an enormous operation we were undertaking. But everyone was so eager to help out, that it went fine.

The different organizations that were willing to donate some prepared food helped out a lot. We were running breakfast, lunch and supper from the kitchen, plus sending out sandwiches. The Red Cross had me handling the food donations. They'd take messages and tell people, "Debbie will get back to you later." That helped a lot because I didn't want everything coming in at one time. I was also running out of walk-in cooler space. Thankfully, our new kitchen was done. Having the freezer and cooler there was a real blessing. Even with both of them, it was still very crowded.

We needed to keep track of all the sandwiches we were making, so we kept a count of how many we put into each pan, and wrote those figures on a piece of paper outside the walk-in cooler door. Each sandwich had to be individually wrapped, but the workers in the kitchen were so good they had no problem with this. Each day there were new workers. Siren School staff members showed up to help out every day. One day, we made 4,000 sandwiches.

Each morning, we would get a call to let us know roughly how many volunteers were working around the area at various work stations. That helped us get an idea of how much packaged food—like chips, crackers, fruit, granola bars—we had to send out. I had signs listing each drop site on a wall down one hallway at school. When the call came in, we would put everything together and place the food for each drop site under its sign. When the person for that site came in to pick up the food, we would go into the walk-in cooler and grab some sandwiches. Then they would go out to the semi-trailer and get their beverages. From there, they'd go over to another truck to pick up some ice.

We also had people just driving around giving food to people. I had a book at my little table, where I kept note of where people were going and at what time. That was to make sure we didn't have different people going to the same area. We had lots of people wanting to make deliveries, but it was very hard to tell them where to go if they weren't from the area because a lot of the street signs, landmarks and buildings were gone. So we'd tell them just to take the food, and give it to anyone they saw who needed it.

If people were familiar with a certain area, then we'd send them there to see what was needed. I kept track of what they told me. I did have a plat book and picked out some places that I knew had been hit. Every couple of days, or whenever needed, the Emergency Response Team, Siren Methodist Church Pastor Steve Ward, the Red Cross, the Salvation Army and myself would meet about what was happening. Some days there were meetings with others. It was all very interesting.

The days were long, but there was so much going on that the time went very fast. No day was the same. I didn't know from one minute to the next what was around the corner—from unloading a truck, to answering the phone, to cooking food, to helping someone find the Red Cross or Salvation Army. I was always very busy, but didn't mind it a bit. I knew that was my way of helping the town.

My family was very supportive. My husband, Jim Jaskolka, works for the village, and was also putting in lots of hours helping out. My son, Derek, and daughter, Brittany, were with my niece, Heather O'Brien, making deliveries on a four-wheeler all day long, every day. From taking rolls in the morning, to sandwiches in the afternoon and evenings, they put in long hours, too, right alongside everyone else. The four-wheeler proved very handy because it could get into places that a vehicle couldn't. They felt that was a way they could help out, and indeed it was. God bless them, and everyone else, for all their hard work.

Whenever we would run low on something, someone always seemed to respond right away with a fresh supply. Ice was one thing we always seemed to need because we went through so much of it keeping food and drinks cold. We were using over 24 coolers ourselves, plus those people brought in on their own. The ice companies did a great job. Another time, we had no cheese to make sandwiches, but once we put the word out, we had plenty right away. It was great to see the response. Then came the day we had no bread or buns. When I told the Red Cross, they ordered 1,000 loaves of bread, plus 1,000 trays of buns. We figured that would hold us over for a while.

I was always wondering where I'd put everything, but I never turned down a donation because I knew I'd find a place once we had it. The way we were going through food, we would most certainly need everything we could get. And it was nice to have a variety of things to give people to eat.

There are so many organizations and business that donated—I have a record of more than 200—I'm afraid to mention names because I don't want anyone to feel their donation wasn't appreciated, because, believe me, it was. The churches and organizations around the area were also great. They all helped out a lot—from making sandwiches, to bringing hot dishes to baking cookies and bars. I can't thank people enough.

When it first started, we were open 24 hours a day; we were preparing food all the time. We had four tables of food for people. We didn't want anyone to go away hungry. I figured they shouldn't have to worry about that, given everything else they had to handle.

KQRS Radio in the Twin Cities and Cub Foods did a food drive, and brought in two semi-trailers. General Mills also sent two trailers filled with food. Trio Paper donated a semi load of paper products. Many other organizations also sent loads of donated goods. Volunteers spent a lot of time unloading and sorting items that we so desperately needed. Some businesses pledged financial support through Sysco Foods. The company's local salesman, Mike Sogge, would then come to me and tell me how much money we had. That was very helpful because I could use that money to order items we needed that hadn't been donated.

My day would start about 5:00 in the morning, and I'd keep going until about midnight. There was so much to get done—from organizing things, to making phone calls, to making sure we had enough lunchmeat for the next day. One thing I never had to worry about: finding enough volunteers to man the kitchen. We had anywhere from 25 to 35 people there every day—some were in town on vacation, others came just to help out. What wonderful people we have here in the United States. We had volunteers from 23 different states.

I don't want to leave out the young men from ALERT (Air Land Emergency Resource Team). Everyone enjoyed having them around. They would eat breakfast at 6:00 A.M., and then spend the whole day out working. After supper in the evening, they would go right back to work if we needed them to do anything, from unloading trucks to going and getting ice. They slept in the gym at night. It was very hot in there, but they never complained about a thing. It was sad to see them leave.

I would like to give a special thank you to Siren Schools Superintendent Jim Bucher and all the Siren School staff for everything they did to make my job easier. It was greatly appreciated. I might not have told you at the time, but now I am putting it in writing: THANKS SO MUCH. GOD BLESSES EACH ONE OF YOU.

Together, by early July, we served or delivered nearly 100,000 meals—and that doesn't even include the food we gave out the night of the tornado!

Editor's Note: Although Debbie is much too modest to say it herself, many people I have spoken to since the tornado give her credit for keeping the operation at the school running so smoothly, and have commended her for the long hours she put in day after day.

The Hand of God

"I thank God for all the special people who have come to help and have left footprints on our hearts forever as they shared their love with us."

—*Pastor Steve Ward, Siren and Lewis United Methodist Church*

By Pastor Steve Ward

As I look back with the advantage of thirteen weeks behind us, I could ask myself where was God when this tornado struck? But instead I say where is it that God wasn't? In life we always look back, and can see God's hand at work even if we didn't realize it at the time.

This is how I saw God at work, as I worked with the many people I know God put in place to help with the emergency crisis and relief after the tornado.

God was there long before the storm, as our police chief, Dean Roland, went around trying to warn people that a storm was coming. God was there as people took shelter.

God was there as Phil Stromberg, a Wisconsin Department of Natural Resources Forest Ranger from Webster, used a plan the night of the tornado that he had developed to help firemen get to fires in an emergency. That plan proved critical as the DNR stepped in to help right from the beginning, and in the weeks after, cutting and brushing many of the trees that the tornado blew over. Many trees had to be cut the night of the storm to help emergency

people get to trapped victims, as well as electrical people through the debris to help restore the power with the many downed power lines.

God was there when Burnett County Emergency Management Director Bobbi Sichta coordinated the overall recovery effort.

God was there when this community passed a building project for a new elementary school, cafeteria and school auditorium. This facility was used after the tornado as a shelter for people whose homes were lost or damaged. The cafeteria was used to feed the people and the many volunteers who came to help our town. It was also a gathering place for people to come and share their stories. Red Cross, Salvation Army, Federal Emergency Management Agency (FEMA) and Social Services all set up there to be in one place for the people who were affected by the tornado, so they could come and get help. The auditorium was used to hold a community prayer service for people to gather together and pray and share their stories. How wonderful that we can come together ecumenically as God's people!

God was there when the school administration and staff answered the call to the community's great need at a time of crisis. God was there, many years ago, when the school district hired Debbie Jaskolka to run the school kitchen. After the tornado, Debbie gave countless hours of her own time to coordinate the volunteer effort to keep people fed. Other school staff pitched in and helped.

God was there when the St. Croix Tribe responded and wanted to share in the recovery.

God is still there and continuing his blessing as many organizations and volunteers from all over continue to come and work. Some offer prayer and financial support. God continues to help by sending the United Methodist Committee on Relief, Christian Aid Ministries, United Methodist Volunteers in Mission, Church of the Brethren and Lutheran Social Services. These Church organizations, as well as many other people, are all working together to share God's love by helping God's people.

God is here now with Project Recovery and The Community Interfaith Connection (CIC). God is here working with these people as the community and the whole area continues to heal and rebuild. How nice that the community, churches, school, chamber of commerce, village employees and government agencies can all work together. People who provide disaster relief all over the country commented how nice it was to see us all work together.

I thank God that this was a close community before the storm. Since the storm, and because of the storm, we have grown closer together. We have come together at community dinners to love and support each other, and we have found that good does come out of bad times. Our faith is stronger, and we will, with God's help, continue to rebuild this wonderful community.

Where was God?

God was before us, getting this great group of people ready. God is beside us to guide and comfort us. God is there in the future saying, "You can do all things through Christ who gives us the strength." (*Philippians 4:13*)

I thank God for giving us hope, strength, and comfort in this time. I thank God for all the special people who have come to help and have left footprints on our hearts forever as they shared their love with us.

God Bless you all.
Your brother in Christ,
Pastor Steve Ward,
Siren and Lewis United Methodist Church

Bringing Comfort

"I think praying together and working together helped us through."

—*Rev. Patricia Baglien, whose community was hit by a tornado in 1998*

by Nancy Jappe

Twenty-four people from the city of Comfrey, Minnesota, 75 percent of which was destroyed by a tornado in 1998, made a special visit to Siren in late September. They came to share food, hugs, prayers and words of encouragement with victims of the June 18 tornado that slammed through a 41-mile, 6-block-wide path in Burnett and Washburn counties.

Following their tornado which created a 1-1/4-mile-wide path of destruction, the people of Comfrey received so much money in donations that they could set aside some for other uses. Sharing with people who had a similar experience was one of those uses.

The people from Comfrey know how important it is to hear from other tornado survivors during difficult times. Residents from Chandler, Minnesota, which was hit by a tornado five years earlier, visited Comfrey after the tornado there. "They came to us and said, 'You are going to make it. We made it. You are going to make it.' Their words meant so much," commented Rev. Patricia Baglien, in Siren on behalf of the Comfrey Ministerium.

Her church, New Hope Lutheran Church, is a combination of two churches—a German Lutheran Church on one end of town and a Swedish Lutheran Church on the other end—both destroyed by the tornado. During the rebuilding process, the two congregations worshipped and had meals at the Catholic Church, which was not damaged. "I think praying together and working together helped us through," Rev. Baglien said.

There were no deaths in Comfrey as the result of the tornado, and only one injury. The buildings in town were older buildings, and were only insured for what they were worth before the tornado. Finding out how little insurance could be applied to rebuilding homes and businesses was a shock to the people of Comfrey, as it has been to people in the Siren area.

The first anniversary of the tornado was a big day in Comfrey. As always, when the people there get together, they had a meal and fellowship. Everybody was given a red rose. The roses meant progress on the road to rebuilding. The recipients were told to give the rose to some-body who needed a rose. "We found doing something concrete to mark the day, or doing something important, to be very helpful," the pastor said.

Lyle Haseltine (R), brother of tornado victim Tom Haseltine, and his wife, Shirley, were greeted by Rev. Patricia Baglien, New Hope Lutheran Church, Comfrey, Minn., during a lunch in Siren put on by people from Comfrey. On March 29, 1998, 75 percent of the city of Comfrey was destroyed by an F-3/F-4 tornado. The people of Comfrey received so much money in donations that they set aside some for other uses. Sharing with people who had a similar experience was one of them. Photo courtesy of Inter-County Leader.

With Love, From Around the Country

"Money was much needed at this time. It soon came."

—Mary Adeline Boehm, June 12, 1899
The New Richmond Cyclone

As several hundred thousand dollars worth of donations poured into Siren, so did the letters. At both of Siren's banks, Bremer and Firstar, employees posted the notes on the walls for residents to read. Here is a sampling of the many heartfelt messages. Some came from people who had visited the area before, others from survivors of tornados elsewhere. And then there were those from people who had simply heard about the Siren tornado on the news and felt compelled to give. Judy Johnson, treasurer of the Siren Tornado Relief Fund at Firstar Bank, is holding some of the letters. Photo courtesy of Inter-County Leader.

Dear folks in Siren,

We've driven through Siren for years on our way to our cabin at Casey Lake. We'd stop for groceries, a bite to eat—always loved the feel of a small town. We were just through a few weeks ago, and missed the little drive-in that was replaced by the Dairy Queen. But took some comfort in the fact we knew it was probably owned by local folks, and there were still all those bright young faces there at the counter. So it was OK.

We were shocked to hear the DQ is gone now too, and so sorry for all the people who lost their homes and businesses. And the trees—we had extensive damage to our home about a year ago when straight-line winds hit Lake Elmo. We're still repairing and picking up the pieces, but we miss the trees the most. Buildings can be rebuilt, but the trees . . .

We are so sorry for the devastation and your loss—this is such a pittance for all the damage, but hope it will add to contributions from many others as well, who have also held Siren dear in their hearts. Siren is the little town we all grew up in—or wish we had. We're afraid to drive through when your streets are open again—but we also know you will grow again, just as you have been doing the last few years. God bless you.

Sincerely,
Carol and Rob Arnold

Bella Vista Community Church
(Interdenominational)
Bella Vista, Arkansas 72714
June 27, 2001

Enclosed you will find a check in the amount of $3,000 to be applied to the Tornado Relief Effort for Siren, Wisconsin. We understand that it will be used to assist those living near the town who suffered significant damage and losses from this tragedy.

In a phone conversation with a member of your staff on June 25, I was given to understand that your bank is the repository for the administration of the recovery and rehabilitation funding efforts. I am sure the community is appreciative of your willingness to accept this fiscal responsibility.

Our church is located in Bella Vista, Arkansas, and we are an interdenominational congregation. We, therefore, of our own volition, are able to identify and donate funds to tragic disasters such as yours. We hope what we have sent will provide some measure of assistance to members of your community.

Our prayers are with your community. We hope too, that our prayers will help bring the necessary resilience, strength and financial assistance to restore and heal those things that made your town a very special place called home.

On behalf of our congregation,
Raymond D. Waier
Chairman, Board of Outreach
Bella Vista Community Church

Enclosed is a check for $50 for the Siren Tornado fund.

I am so sorry for all the suffering and anxiety this has brought upon your residents of Siren. I am 90 years old and unable to volunteer, but I trust this small check will be of help in some way.

Once I had a severe automobile accident and was lying in a roadside-ditch and a woman seemed to appear out of nowhere, put her hand on my head and said: "God is with you." It was as if God had sent his angel to assure me of His presence. That was 12 years ago, and I recovered totally though a pick-up truck had rolled over my car.

Jesus has promised, "I am with you always."

Sincerely,
Elizabeth Branstad
St. Paul, MN

Dear Friends of Siren,

I am so sorry to hear of your loss with the disastrous tornado. The people of St. Peter, MN, experienced an F3 tornado as well in March of 1998. Right now, you must be feeling shock, grief, and a tremendous sense of loss. We share your sorrow.

Please know that things will be right again for you. Time will be needed to heal and rebuild, but you will be alright. As you wander through these broken days, remember that God's love will see you through and that people out in the world care.

Best wishes—one day at a time. Take care of yourselves as best you can.

Sincerely,
Susan Bravelin
St. Peter, MN

These checks are for the tornado relief fund. We were saddened to hear about all the damage.

This is kind of in memory of Joyel Yambrick—She was our son's donor (liver transplant 5/3/94). Also, we'd like to remember Bill and Mary Yambrick and boys Alex and Paul with this donation. It's not much, but we hope it helps.

Thank you!
Barb, Har and Michael Bren

From the Catholic Churches of:

St. Joseph
Osceola, WI 54020
Our Lady of the Lakes
Centuria, WI 54824
St. Patrick
Centuria, WI 54824

To Whom This May Concern:

This past weekend we took up a second collection for the many victims of the Tornado Damaged Area of Siren. These contributions are from the parishioners and visitors of the Catholic Churches of St. Patrick's in Centuria and Our Lady of the Lakes in Balsam Lake.

We trust that these will be distributed according to needs of the area residents. Thank you for all of your work and dedication; we continue to keep everyone in our prayers.

Sincerely In Christ,
Rev. Thomas E. Thompson
Pastor (St. Patrick/Our Lady of the Lakes)

ENC: Check for $1395.64

My thoughts and prayers are with you all in your losses. However, I see by newscasts you are determined to survive. God be with you all!!

Lee Clawson

I am so sorry your town has suffered this tragedy and am happy to contribute to a fund that will help victims. I am too old to contribute physical assistance and hope, in this way, to lend support wherever needed.

Two natural disasters have figured in my life—the 1968 tornado that almost destroyed my hometown, Charles City, IA, where my parents were still living, and the 1989 earthquake in Loma Prieta (San Francisco), CA, where I was living at the time. I know what it was/is like to be without essentials—water, electricity, a roof overhead, etc.—things we take so much for granted.

God bless all of you in this monumental struggle to recover. Faith and hope will carry you through.

Sincerely,
Georgene Draheim

We were sorry about the storm. We have a cabin by Voyager Village and have been coming through Siren for 21 years. We were upset by the damage, but uplifted by everyone's spirit and determination. Put this to good use.

Alan and Lollie Eidsness.
Siren

The little town that could, did and will again!

Our best wishes and prayers as you undertake your rebuilding plans.

Sincerely,
Gary & Mary Haas
A & H Country Market, Inc

To The People of Siren, Wis:

I have never visited your town, but had always heard what a pretty place it is. I'm sure that's a far memory from what we saw on TV this week after the terrible tornado that destroyed so much. I am so sorry for your losses, and can only imagine with tears in my eyes and a lump in my throat all the devastation and shock you had to go through. We thank God most people were safe including my co-worker's aunt Gladys who survived in her bathroom when the entire rest of her home was blown away.

We know that you're not giving up and are already hard at work bringing the town back to life. You are an inspiration to the rest of this country. On the TV news tonight they called your town "Phoenix" rising up from the ashes.

I am enclosing a small check, which by itself can't do much. But I hope that millions of others share my support of your people and help you in a monetary way. I know you've gotten some manual help, too.

All the best to your future. I hope to be able to visit the new Siren soon.

Patty Henry
Bloomington, MN

Our prayers are with you too.

I hope things are going better for the tornado victims. It is so sad to have such a thing happen. Our city had this disastrous flood in 1997. We lost everything also.

Good Luck and God Bless
Maurine Hughes
Grand Forks, ND

Village of Siren

Enclosed is a check for the Tornado Relief fund. I wish it could be more. I have a cabin on the Yellow River and have shopped in your town on many weekends since Aug. 1986. My prayers are with all of your residents and God speed in the rebuilding and recovery of your lovely town.

Sincerely,
Gloria Keith

Dear People of Siren,

Seeing the footage of the damage to your town brought back many memories of the sights, sounds, and smells from the tornado that hit St. Peter on March 29, 1998. Please know that you are all in our thoughts and prayers.

We know that things look pretty bleak right now, but *believe* that things will get better! It has been almost three years since our storm, and all things are not rebuilt. But, what has been done looks wonderful. It will be a long process, but I'm sure you'll appreciate every step.

Please accept this check for your recovery efforts. Feel free to use the money towards any project you see fit—be it trees, your ice arena, individual needs, etc.

Keep your chins up and God bless you all.
Rob and Nancy Larson
St. Peter, MN

The employees of McKesson Medical in Golden Valley, Minnesota, have taken up a collection for the victims of the devastating tornado; we wish it could have been more. Our employees send their sincere good wishes to everyone in Siren and hope that funds will continue to pour in to the community for recovery and restoration.

Best regards
Rose Johnson
Director, Facilities
McKesson Corporation

This will be our 9th year that we'll be driving through your community. We have truly enjoyed seeing your progress in improving your lovely town and area.

Of course, this year will be another story. We are deeply saddened by the horrible devastation you folks have encountered. Can't imagine how you cope with it all. Guess tragedy does bring people closer together and that surely must be your salvation—along with a trust in God.

The enclosed money *was* earmarked for a local charity, but when my husband and I saw the destruction you folks are going through, we immediately decided to divert the funds to you folks in Siren.

Know that you are in our thoughts and prayers.
Duane and Mary Jo Russ

Enclosed you will find a small gift to be shared with our Siren neighbors.

We celebrated our 35th wedding anniversary last week, and I had a thought during my morning devotions. We (my bride and I) do not need more stuff or shelves to put *stuff* on. We both agreed we would be happier to share our gifts that God has given us. Please find $35.00 (one dollar for each year that God has given us together). May He now give the people of Siren gifts of money, strength, and hope—and most of all *FAITH*.

We love you Siren,
Denny and Linda Splatt

The Voices of Children

Along with the adults in the Siren area, many children were also deeply affected by the tornado and its aftermath. They, too, have stories to share. On the following pages, some children tell us in their own words, and through pictures they created, how the tornado impacted them.

By Donna Tjader

I teach second grade in the Siren School District. Today is September 7th, almost 11 weeks after the tornado hit Siren. Still, when it rains and thunders, as it did today, I notice a great deal of anxiety in one of my students. He couldn't participate in class activities because he was too nervous, and had to come and sit with me while I read to him. I have a class of 13 students, and 3 of them lost their homes in the tornado.

When we resumed summer school one week after the tornado, we had "Tornado Talk" time each day. The boys and girls had so many stories to tell, and seemed so relieved that someone wanted to listen to them. They seemed to be coping quite well, although one of my students sat at his desk and pulled the hair out of his head. He was one of the unfortunate students whose home had been destroyed. He needed to see the counselor right away.

I see a broad range of emotions among the children, with most seeming okay and ready to resume a more normal life. However, I am concerned about days like today when we have stormy weather, and also about next April when we do our Tornado Awareness activities. This may bring back painful memories.

We will be running support groups for the students, with Project Recovery counselors coming in to help. Tornado coloring books have been given to all of the children and there has been some "Tornado Talk" time, but I am striving to make things as normal as possible in the classroom, and not dwell on the storm.

Following are stories told by Donna Tjader's students:

By Christina Luna

Our neighbors told us that a tornado was coming. All of the kids were telling the adults, "A tornado is going to happen!" There was green coming down from the sky. None of the windows were broke. My neighbor's windshield fell off. They had to get a new one. After the tornado, we couldn't get out of the door so we had to stay in the house until somebody helped us. I felt very scared that I had to squeeze my kitten. It sounded like glass was breaking. Siren looked like trash!

By Isaac Wegner

I was in my van, and my dad was under a craft table. I helped my dad clean up. One of my dad's employees called my dad and told him to get in the basement. It sounded very loud. The clouds were in strips. It looked like a T-Rex came through Siren! My house and my dad's shop were destroyed. We found my dog about one-third of a mile away. He had one leg broken and two sprained. The vet couldn't help him because he was too banged up so he died. I am very sad.

By Ian Martin

The tornado was about a half mile away from my house and it took us five hours to get back home. We were in Hertel when the tornado hit. When we stopped at a gas station the wind was like a hurricane. When we got to Siren we were stuck with trees blocking, and telephone wires blocking the road. And that is why it took us five hours to get home.

By Jordan Sargent

We went shopping. I was riding with my grandpa, and we stopped at the stop sign. We were down in my basement. My grandpa was lucky because he dropped to the ground out in our garage. My grandma was scared! My dog must have been scared, too, because he didn't lick me at all. The tornado sounded like a train passing by. I was scared and so was A.J. He wanted to be by grandma.

By Tyler Richison

My neighbors chose the right bathroom because when the tornado was over, the bathroom was the only thing left. I was coming home from Spooner when the clouds were going all different directions and my mom yelled at my dad, "Jim, you better get in the hotel now!" So we stopped at The Lodge. My house was wrecked so we are living with my grandma and grandpa right now.

This is a poem I wrote about my new house:

I'm waiting
For furniture to be sat on
For bedding to be bought
For shingles to be put on the roof
For carpet to be vacuumed
For games to be played
And then I'll know
It's time to move into my new house!

By Travis Nadeau

At first my mom, sister, and I hid in our bathroom. We heard on the news that a tornado was coming. It sounded like giants were jumping on our roof! We ran across the street to our neighbor's basement. I never saw my mom run so fast! She was scared! The roof flew off of our house, my brother's window fell off, and there was a hole in my mom's wall. When the tornado ended we had to walk to my grandma's house, over all the trees and telephone poles. We found mom's santa in the "S-Pond" through the woods. A bulldozer knocked the rest of our house down. Siren looks like a giant bowling ball came through it!

By Tayler Frederickson

My house almost broke down because the tornado almost broke our house, but it decided to go through town. I was in my basement. The sky looked icky brown and green. I felt scared that it might break my house down. We went to the theatre after the tornado to see if my grandma was okay, but we couldn't get through because there were power lines in the way, but we jumped over one. My grandma was okay because the police got them out right away.

By Jessica Lysdahl

I went to Mark's house because we don't have a basement. There were warnings on the TV. Our lights went off one time. Our pine tree fell down. I went to my grandma's house after the tornado. My mom was at work when the tornado came. My mom came to grandma's house after work. I felt scared.

By Kaylene Johnson

I don't live in Siren, but there are some things I miss, like the Dairy Queen. When it was storming and we looked outside one side of the house was sunny and one side was cloudy!

By Sara Long

My antenna broke off. My step dad was sitting by the window and my mom was screaming and so was my brother. Siren looks like a disaster. It sounded like a big cloud rolling down the road. I felt sad as can be.

By Allison Oustigoff

Chad went to the theatre with Monica when the tornado happened. When my auntie looked up she saw the tornado. She thought it looked like an ice cream cone!

By Gage Lindemann

I was up in my bedroom playing. I went downstairs and saw the tornado warning on TV. I went to tell my mom about the warning. She came quickly to see the warning on the TV. We took some candles, blankets, and chairs and went to the basement. We stayed there until it was safe. When I got upstairs some trees were knocked over in our driveway, but we were safe!

By Rachel Gloodt

My Aunt Dawn and Uncle Tom came with my Grandma Shirley and Grandpa Jerry and my Aunt Arlene because they lost their power. My Uncle Red's barn got smashed in the tornado. My Uncle Tom was washing the Zamboni at the hockey arena. The people didn't show up for the meeting so he went home. That was a good thing or he might have been in the tornado!

A Scary Time

"The tornado isn't my friend."

—*Abigail Mitchell, 7-year-old Siren Resident*

By Abigail Mitchell

Everyday is a good day except for the days of the tornado. The day of the tornado was scary. We were at my grandma's house. I was holding on to my cat very hard because I was very scared. My cat was scratching me, but I didn't care because I love him. We slept at Grandma and Grandpa Howe's house.

Andi called the next day and I wanted to call Leanne and Taylor, but I didn't know their number, so I couldn't call them. I wanted to forget about the tornado. I am still scared today. My mom said it would take a while to forget, so I try to plug my ears when it storms. One night it was a wind storm.

It was a nice summer day until the night of the tornado. I didn't like the night of the tornado because I lost my house and I haven't seen my friends, only one of them, Brittany. Me and my friends haven't seen each other since the last day of school. I like my friends and the tornado isn't my friend because I can't get there because it has so much wind. I like my class because they are my friends and they are good friends. Do you know why? Because I'm supposed to like them. I am going into 2nd grade. I miss 1st grade. The End.

(Seven-year-old Abigail Mitchell is Siren resident Rosie Howe's daughter.)

Photo courtesy of St. Paul Pioneer Press.

Seasons Without Shade

"This generation will never see New Richmond clothed in its foliage beauty as it was arrayed before the awful cyclone robbed it of its many attractions. Yet time can do much, so let us hope for brighter days."

—Mary Adeline Boehm, June 12, 1899
The New Richmond Cyclone

Trees

I think that I shall never see
A poem lovely as a tree.

A tree whose hungry mouth is prest
Against the earth's sweet flowing breast;

A tree that looks at God all day,
And lifts her leafy arms to pray;

A tree that may in Summer wear
A nest of robins in her hair;

Upon whose bosom snow has lain;
Who intimately lives with rain.

Poems are made by fools like me,
But only God can make a tree.

Joyce Kilmer
(1886–1918)

Missing the Trees

"It is just hard. I still find it hard to get up in the morning and see nothing."

—*Laverne Lauder, Tornado Victim*

by Nancy Jappe

The landscape in Burnett County changed drastically in the space of seconds Monday, June 18. Trees that had been standing proudly and majestically for over 100 years were left toppled, twisted, devoid of leaves and leaning against roofs, houses, cars and other trees. Today, when people talk about the tornado, it's most often about how they miss the trees; realizing they won't see big mature trees in their lifetime like the ones they lost.

The Lauder children's cabin before the storm.

No one feels the loss of the trees more than LaVerne and Gordon Lauder. The Lauders lost between eight and nine acres of white pine on that memorable night in June. The trees were planted in 1941 and some were between 50 and 70 feet tall. None are left now. The property they were on in the Town of LaFollette east of Siren had been in Gordon's family for nearly 100 years. Eighty-year-old Gordon and 78-year-old LaVerne retired to that property from Illinois 23 years ago.

LaVerne, LaFollette town clerk until two years ago, had been at a town meeting June 18. The word went out that a tornado was due to strike Siren at 8:30 P.M. LaVerne was worried, knowing that Gordon often went night fishing. That is, in fact, where he had been; however, he and LaVerne arrived home at the same time.

Gordon was pouring himself a cup of coffee when he saw a greenish-black cloud come across Warner Lake, followed by the roar that is usually associated with a tornado. The Lauders only had time to get into a hallway before the tornado passed by. "It was over in 15 seconds," LaVerne recalled. "We weren't even knocked down. We were just standing there together. The first we knew, we could hear the sound of trees falling."

Before they even realized the extent of the trees that had fallen, the Lauders looked across 150–200 feet to where their children's summer home had been. All that was left of the home—

This is all that was left of the children's summer home about 150–200 feet from the Lauder home after the June 18 tornado hit. The missing home was the first thing the Lauders noticed when they came up from their basement after the tornado.

former cabin for Gordon's parents from the 1940s and completely remodeled by their son, Scott—was the fireplace. But that was only the beginning of the devastation the Lauders faced, complicated by the fact that their driveway was blocked, and their telephone was out. For awhile they just sat there, wondering what to do.

The first task was to get some plastic to block off broken windows and some tarp to stop the rain that was coming into one of the bedrooms. Then Gordon ran to his car radio (in the garage under the house). Gordon is a member of NorWesCo RACES, the amateur radio group that is active in the area. He was able to get through to LaFollette Town Chairman Ed Jacobsen, who is also a member of RACES. By 11 P.M., the Lauders could see light at the end of their driveway, which is a quarter mile into the woods.

It took from 11 P.M. to 2:30 A.M. for members of the St. Croix Hertel Fire Department (led by John Taylor) to get to the Lauders, who were able to stay the night in the house. The next morning, they were able to get the car out of the garage and head out to find a telephone to notify their family.

"It is just hard. I still find it hard to get up in the morning and see nothing," LaVerne said. "Gordon was young when (the cabin) was built. Our children, grandchildren and now great-grandchildren have been coming up from Illinois (to enjoy the place)." Air-conditioning became a must, with all the shade from the trees gone. This was something the Lauders never thought they would need.

"We lost our trees but we have our home. We will survive," LaVerne said.

Logging as result of the tornado

According to Wisconsin Department of Natural Resources (DNR) Ranger Phil Stromberg, 7,400 acres of timber, most of it on privately owned land like the Lauders' property, were affected by the June 18 tornado. This number does not include trees that were outside the high-impact area.

"Everything in the way went," Stromberg said, "aspen, oak, jack pine and red pine plantations, large mature majestic (trees) in the Warner and Little Bass lakes area." Stromberg said the DNR's role in the cleanup of private land is to communicate and coordinate the work of forestry consultants, the ones the DNR depends on to get the job done. There are three in the area: Paul Noreen from Siren, and Dan Cobb and Jeff Groeschel from Hayward. Part of the coordination includes finding out about problems that need to be dealt with, and mediating when people are not happy or their expectations are not entirely in line with the work being done.

"The best way to protect landowners is for an agent to act in their behalf," Stromberg said. Eighty percent of the homeowners are going through forestry consultants; the other 20 percent are using individual loggers. At the time this article was written in early October, 100 cutting permits had been issued. When the landowner signs a permit, it gives the DNR a way to know what is going on, who is cutting and where. It also prevents delinquent properties from getting logged off, when the taxes are overdue. "If taxes are owed, the owner cannot cut," Stromberg said. Using the cutting permits is also a way for the DNR to keep track of which consultant is working in which township. Of the 7,400 acres that were heavily impacted by the tornado, 70 percent has been committed to logging.

The pressure to get the logging done quickly is affected by three factors: the danger for forest fires in the spring, invasion of insects that will affect the value of the wood, and the loss of moisture and weight as the trees dry out.

The DNR is particularly worried about the fire danger in areas where not much timber has been salvaged, which means there is more downed timber left to burn. If a fire were to start in any of these areas, a DNR bulldozer wouldn't be able to get through.

Stromberg pointed to the full-tree chipping operation being done by loggers like T & T Logging as one of the best ways to prevent forest fires. When loggers use this process, they first use a machine that makes chips of the entire tree, from top to bottom. Once the tree is chipped, the chips are all removed. From a fire standpoint, this mean that nothing is left on the ground that would be a fire hazard. "Where T&T goes, they are done. There is no fire hazard. The landowners are presented with a clean site," he said. This is in contrast to leaving slash, as is done when the land is not full-tree chipped.

The DNR will be increasing its fire-prevention training with local fire departments over the winter. They will be working on hazard-mitigation plans to deal with the leftover slash after logging is finished. They have applied to the Federal Emergency Management Agency for funds to create 150 feet of free space around dwellings, at no cost to homeowners in the tornado area. They will also develop a plan to create fuel breaks by treating the slash on both sides of a road at strategic locations, the objective being to stop the fire on the road. (This process involves using a roller chopper to run over all the flammable branches along a roadside. The machine then packs the residue into the soil, again removing potential fire danger.)

Oak Road, in the hardest hit area in the Town of LaFollette, where full-tree chipping has been done, presents a natural fuel break. The village of Siren on the west, Clam Lake, Cranberry, Little Bass and Warner lakes, and the agriculture land in the towns of Dewey and Bashaw are also natural fuel breaks.

For the next 18 months, the DNR will be implementing plans to deal with the danger of forest fire. "By the spring of 2003, we expect to have this problem pretty much finished," Stromberg said.

A Painful Loss

"I lost them all. When they went, part of my life did, too."

—Siren Resident Florence Nelson, talking about the trees ripped from her yard

By Jill Gloodt

Eighty-year-old Florence Nelson has lived her entire life in rural Burnett County, spending nearly 55 of those years in Siren. She can recall what it was like before Siren had streetlights. To Florence it's a perfect little town; she's always just hated it when people have something bad to say about Siren.

For 33 years she was married to Bob Nelson. "We lived each day as a gift," she recalls, "We were so lucky to have had each other for as long as we did." Bob had passed away in 1974. But Florence still lived in the house they had moved to their lot in town in 1947, and added onto after that. It held many wonderful memories of their times together. The yard was special, too. It held the big, beautiful pine and maple trees she and Bob had planted 53 years ago.

The day of the storm seemed very typical to Florence. She had watched the news until 7:00 P.M., and didn't see any warnings, but 15 minutes later, the electricity went off. She went to the front door and opened it to look out. Florence saw hailstones the size of oranges, and the trees bending. The strong wind made a whooshing sound. The breaking trees

sounded like cannons. It was like WWI and WWII combined.

At this point, She wasn't thinking, just reacting. She walked to the closet under the stairs and stayed there. When it was over—she doesn't remember how long it was—she "checked to see if I was all together. I was and thought that's most important." She gathered her thoughts and got up to look. Her bedroom was covered in glass and lying on her bed was a 7-8 foot tree. She was so shaken up, it took her two days to settle down.

Her friends, Ernie and Bev Swanson, came to check on her shortly after the storm had passed. Florence said she was okay. Her roof was badly damaged, but she didn't care. She wasn't going anywhere. She stayed that first night in her own house. Although her children didn't agree, Florence had decided there wasn't any good reason to leave her house. "They were mad at me for staying," Florence says. "(But) why should I leave? I'm as stubborn as a mule." Her daughter, Judy Anderson, stayed there with her that night.

After spending the next couple of nights at

her son's cabin, Florence went back to her house, and made do with what she had. While there was a generator, she didn't have any lights for 9 1/2 days. She couldn't sleep on her bed, so she slept on the couch.

Less than two months later, her house was pretty much back together. Looking better than it did before, she said. The toughest part for Florence has been losing all but two of her trees. Her shady yard is gone. "It sticks out like a sore thumb now. I lost them all. When they went, part of my life did, too."

Gordon and Marian Ackland, Siren, donated 100 Colorado blue spruce trees to the village as part of the Tournament for the Trees that was held at Siren Glen Golf Course. The Acklands have been growing trees since 1983. "I think they will lend something to the village," Gordon said. "They go with the (northwoods atmosphere of the) town," Marian added. Photo courtesy of Inter-County Leader.

The Gift

"The bigger the trees that are moved, the sooner they will make an impact in town."

—Siren Resident Gordon Ackland, on the reason he and his wife are donating trees to the community

by Nancy Jappe

Gordon and Marian Ackland, who grow Colorado blue spruce trees on their 16-acre property a mile west of Siren, are donating 100 of the trees as part of the Tournament for the Trees being sponsored by the Siren Glen Golf Course Monday, Sept. 24. "We are trying to leave some beauty in the world before we have to leave it," Gordon explained.

The Acklands are not golfers; they are tree lovers. After reading in the newspaper about the golf tournament and the proceeds that are to go totally to replacing trees lost in the June 18 tornado, they decided to make the donation.

The trees will be moved into the village of Siren next spring. Their height will be between 8 and 12 feet. "Trees that have some size and will be more showy," Gordon said. "We are growing these trees because we think they are the most beautiful trees out there. The bigger the trees that are moved, the sooner they will make an impact in town."

The Acklands started in the tree business back in 1983 because they wanted to do something with a field of weeds behind their house.

They just couldn't stand looking at those weeds any longer.

The first seedlings they bought came in as 6-inch sticks from a nursery in Michigan. The sticks were planted in the garden behind the house, where they were left to grow for the next two years. When the trees were two years old, they were replanted into another part of the garden. After being there a while, they were replanted for a third time out in the field.

"Stretching the wire to make straight rows is the hardest part of the planting," Marian commented, adding that she and Gordon worked hard on the planting. The process includes digging a hole, filling the hole full of peat to help with moisture retention, providing a means for water runoff, fertilizing and watering. Dry weather and pocket gophers are natural enemies of the growing trees.

According to Gordon, the trees don't grow much during the first year. After they have developed a good root system, however, they will grow about two feet a year.

For the past six years, the Ackland nursery has been shipping Colorado blue spruce to

Aspen, Colorado. The trees are not native to Colorado, and the Acklands aren't sure where the name comes from. What they do know is that this is the only specie of tree that will survive in the weather around Aspen. This means they will do well in the Wisconsin climate, too.

In the biggest shipping season so far, the nursery sent out about 22 carloads of trees, with about 25 trees per carload. Women from the Danbury area come in to sew the burlap around the base of the trees. There can be as many as 24 people in the yard at a time, balling up dirt around the base and tacking down the burlap protector.

Fraser fir, a tree native to North Carolina, is also grown in the Ackland nursery. This species of tree also does well in the Wisconsin winter climate. Because this is a licensed nursery, inspectors come around every year to ensure the quality of the trees the Acklands grow.

Growing spruce and fir, "there are no leaves to rake," Gordon said, with a smile on his face. The Acklands lost all the trees in the front of their house when crews widened Highway 70 about six years ago. Undaunted, they moved a whole line of 10- to 12-foot trees to the front of the house. Those trees have grown at least to a height of 18 feet now. They are particularly mourning the loss of 10 feet on the top of one of the biggest trees during the June 18 tornado. "We were so proud of that tree," Marian said.

Gordon was the only one home on June 18, the night the tornado raced through Burnett County. He was out in the yard, watching its approach until branches and debris started flying. Although he was only three feet from the house, it took forever for him to get inside. "It felt like I was in a vacuum," he said.

The Acklands are happy about their decision to donate the 100 spruce trees to the village of Siren. They have a little concern over the move next spring, saying that the right equipment needs to be used, and somebody must be ready to plant and take care of the trees once they are in their new location. Because of the size of the trees, a lot of watering will be necessary if Mother Nature doesn't provide the moisture.

"Property owners who get trees on their boulevard will have to do some watering," Gordon advised. "That will be necessary as we want every one to survive. They will, if the (process) is done property."

"Tender loving care, TLC, that is what is needed," Marian added.

Editor's Note: This article reprinted with permission from the Inter-County Leader newspaper.

Comforting Thoughts

"The city is today rising from its ruins."

—*Mary Adeline Boehm, June 12, 1899*
The New Richmond Cyclone

The House North of Town

"The house is gone, but our memories of THE HOUSE NORTH OF TOWN will go on forever."

—*Nina Borup Malmen*

By Nina Borup Malmen

We all have somewhere in the back of our minds, the home of our dreams. For my folks, (Olof and Fannie Borup) this dream home became a reality when they bought an old, vacant, run-down home north of Falun, Wisconsin. (Falun is 6 miles west of Siren.) It was purchased in the mid-50s, at a cost of $500.

According to my dictionary the word weather-beaten is defined as being seasoned, worn, stained, or warped by exposure to weather. This house met the requirements of all of these descriptions.

During the early years of ownership we continued to live in the rooms behind our restaurant known as "Fannie's Kitchen" which was located on Highway 70 in the little town of Falun. THE HOUSE NORTH OF TOWN served as a storage place for some of our furniture and off-season clothing.

For a period of time it was rented to a large family. That did not work out very well. They did not take care of the property, and they ate all of the applesauce that my mother had stored in the root cellar. Her comment was, she supposed, "That they were hungry."

Customers of the restaurant would frequently inquire as to what my folks would do when they retired. They had the answer. "We will move to THE HOUSE NORTH OF TOWN." This dream came true in 1961 when they sold the restaurant and had THE HOUSE NORTH OF TOWN "fixed-up" and it finally became their long-awaited dream home.

I once asked my mother, "How many acres of land do you have? Her answer was, "About as much as you can see." Whatever the amount there was enough for a spacious yard, beautiful flower beds and the necessary space for the all-important garden.

Giving directions to THE HOUSE NORTH OF TOWN was easy. It was just across the road from the Northwestern Wisconsin Substation and just south of the Falun Ballpark. A small building which served as the garage and my dad's shop was located north of the house.

As the years passed by THE HOUSE NORTH OF TOWN began to collect various memories. Our photo albums reveal reunions, parties and gatherings for Easter, Thanksgiving and the Christmas Holidays. In our minds we see the small wood-burning stove in the kitchen and the glass-paned doors between the dining and living room.

Life at THE HOUSE NORTH OF TOWN changed forever in July of 1976 when my mother lost her life in a tragic accident on the road that passed by THE HOUSE NORTH OF TOWN.

Recently, I have been informed that the former retirement home of my parents has been reduced to shambles by a tornado. When my dad built the kitchen cabinets in THE HOUSE NORTH OF TOWN—it was remarked that they were so well built that if a tornado ever hit the house, the cabinets would probably remain standing.

The house is gone, but our memories of THE HOUSE NORTH OF TOWN will go on forever.

The wind is blowing, a blizzard is raging, my winter coat is nowhere to be found. Please do not fret or worry, it is probably stored at THE HOUSE NORTH OF TOWN.

Editor's Note: Nina Borup Malmen now lives in Newport, Oregon.

Tornado-inspired Words

"The tired smile, handshake, or hug really says it all."

—Shelly Java, Grantsburg, Wisconsin, Resident

By Shelly Java

I have had many wondrous things happen in my life; writing this poem about the tornado is one of them. I felt I needed to share this with you. Our love and prayers go out to the people in Alpha, Falun, Siren, Hertel, Spooner and Shell Lake. The feelings and hurt do not affect only the immediate area. It ripples out to family, friends, and then to people in other cities and states.

The gratitude is on the tired faces of the people you help after a long day of sawing trees, picking up debris, working at the courthouse or helping at the Salvation Army station. The tired smile, handshake, or hug really says it all:

A storm came through a town one day.
What I saw is so difficult to say.
The broken houses and their precious lives,
The death and destruction of things that were alive,
The twisted and mangled trees,
These are only a few things that I can see.
They say the storm was like a living thing,
Pure evil they say, destruction did it bring.
They say the noise in their ears did roar,
And through the sky they saw things soar.
Some, their worldly possessions they lost,
Some with their lives, they paid the cost.
Death and destruction was in the path.
We were stunned as we saw the aftermath.
The pictures on TV were so compelling,
As the stories of survival people were telling.

As some saw their animals fly by,
And those who felt their house explode into the sky.
Only a minute did it take,
To create such a havoc in its wake.
The people then had no place to go.
They had to find shelter, this they did know.
Friends, and family, all opened their door,
So the people could rest just a little more.
The next day the cleanup began.
The airwaves called, "Volunteers come if you can."
All across the nation, people cried at the sight,
In awe of the storm's awful might.
The volunteers and supplies came from far and near,
Trying to comfort the people's fear.
Red Cross and disaster groups soon came to the town,
Saying, "We won't let these people down."
The volunteers are working ever so hard,
Their hands from metal and brush are very scarred.
The Christian groups came both to work and praise.
The spirits here needed to be raised.
Out of disaster there comes a light of hope,
As the people there really start to cope.
God's hand was evident on the lives of the people,
When we saw the cross, not moved on the top of the steeple.
God was at work even before the storm came.
Moving people to safety, almost like pawns in a game.
Businesses are opening, some may not again.
The damage and loss were too much for them.
On Wednesday the people, 300, did gather,
To praise the Lord for surviving the weather.
All denominations came to worship the Lord.
The churches in town lost only a few boards.
You cannot tell me out of all this,
That the hand of God this town missed.
The miracles are happening all the time,
Even when this storm came and committed such a crime.
But out of the storm comes a silver lining,
It has showed us strangers, their caring love shining.
People are starting to rebuild and look to the future.

It will be so different, not what they were used to.
This has opened many of the people's eyes.
To see how close to death were their lives.
Why cling to all the possessions of the past?
They are things that may not last.
We are praying that through all of this,
That lives will be saved and not missed.
God knows what has happened and cries for all.
But we have seen and heard his merciful call.

Editor's Note: Shelly Java lives in Grantsburg, Wisconsin, 15 miles west of Siren. Shelly wrote her first poem the day before the tornado, Sunday, June 17. Since the tornado, she has written more than 30 poems. "Like opening the floodgate," she said, describing the flow of words the tornado released in her.